Things That Fall
and Other Chris Walker Stories

E D W A R D M E L T O N

ISBN 979-8-89309-211-0 (Paperback)
ISBN 979-8-89309-212-7 (Digital)

Covenant Books
11661 Hwy 707
Murrells Inlet, SC 29576
www.covenantbooks.com

Things That Fall

She lay on top of the boulder overlooking the game trail. She was watching the path that passed through the tall evergreens and underbrush downslope to a stream where animals came for water. Only her eyes moved as she lay quietly in the dappled predawn light, waiting.

She smelled them before she saw them. The two mule deer, a doe and a yearling, walked down the trail, gradually materializing along the shaded path. The doe led as they watchfully and quietly made their way downhill toward the creek some distance below. They came to a stop not far from the boulder pile, looking around nervously, sensing something. The doe raised her head, sniffed the air, and smelling nothing that she could identify as threatening, lowered her head to graze on a clump of grass among the stones. She stopped, looked over her shoulder at the yearling, turned, and resumed eating. The cougar launched, her body tracing a shallow arc through the air, the powerful thrust of her haunches vaulting her eighty-pound mass of lean muscle over twenty-five feet onto the back of the doe. The claws on the cat's front paws sunk into the shoulders of the deer who bleated most pitifully for a moment, thrashing from side to side, trying to throw this pain-inflicting creature off her back, until the cat's jaws closed on her neck, the fangs paralyzing her, silencing her. They collapsed together onto the pine needles as the horrified yearling wheeled on its back legs and ran back up the trail.

The cougar shook the animal, continuing to grasp it tightly in her jaws. She shook it again, waiting a few moments. She finally released the deer and looked down at it briefly. There was no movement from the dying animal as the light in its wide-open eyes gradually faded. The cat raised her head, gazed around, then grabbed the deer by the neck again. The doe weighed maybe half, again more than the cougar, but she was able to drag the limp animal easily. She dragged it a hundred yards or so, slightly downhill, away from the trail to a spot among the trees where she might hide the carcass…and where she would eat.

*****

Every year, like it or not, he had to make like Paul Bunyan: roaring fires take firewood, and wood fire was the primary source of heat in his home.

The unimproved forest service road meandered among the trees on the hilltop overlooking the valley. The trees were all lodgepole pine, a pure stand. Some had been blown down in recent months or years, and there were standing dead among the healthy trees. The early morning air was clear, the sky cloudless. The high peaks across the valley had a dusting of snow from last night, but heavy snow wouldn't fall for a while yet.

Chris's pickup towed a utility trailer. He had bought forest service permits for cutting wood and needed to top off his supply for the winter. He found an open area and turned the truck around. Shutting off the truck, he walked north, perpendicular to this section of the road. He found several suitable trees and marked them with surveyor's tape. He moved the truck and trailer closer to the marked trees and began offloading his tools. The wheelbarrow came first followed by the case holding his chainsaw, a gas can, and some safety equipment: hard hat, goggles, leather gloves, ear protection, steel-toed boots, and a leather jacket.

His cell phone chirped. He answered, explaining to his wife where he was. She was a little anxious since he was by himself, but the availability of mobile phone service calmed her down a little. She expected him home by midafternoon.

The case holding the chainsaw fell open when he released the plastic clasps. Chris checked the tension on the blade and filled the chain oil reservoir and the gas tank. He donned his protective gear, picked up his saw, and approached the first tree.

The tree had no needles on its bare branches, suggesting that it had been dead awhile, dry enough to burn this year. He walked around the tree, looking up at its shape and its branches. The lowest significant branch was ten feet off the ground. The tree was about forty-five feet high and symmetrical, about a foot in diameter at its base. Chris primed the saw and pulled the starting rope. It started on the third try and clattered along nicely in idle, roaring smoothly when he revved up the engine.

He made his first cut about six inches above and parallel to the ground, cutting the trunk about halfway through. He extracted the blade and made another cut at forty-five degrees to the first, cutting out a wedge of wood. He moved to the other side of the tree and cut into the trunk, nearly meeting the first cut. The tree swayed a little and groaned. Chris shut down the saw and put it on the ground. He leaned against the tree trunk, then jumped back when it began falling away from him, in slow motion initially, accelerating as it neared the ground, where it crashed in a shower of broken limbs, dust, and pine needles. He started the saw again and began cutting logs in about eighteen-inch lengths, trimming branches as he went. He shut off the saw, sat on a thick log, and cleaned the saw blade, letting it cool. He walked back to the truck and found the quart bottle of water lying on his front seat. The clear, cold mountain water tasted wonderful.

Retrieving the wheelbarrow, he began filling it with logs and loading the truck bed. He repeated the process two more times, two more trees, before he stopped to sit down and eat a sandwich.

Two more trees after lunch filled up his truck bed and his trailer. *Maybe a little more than a cord*, he thought. Enough for today.

He cleaned his saw, tightened the chain, and put it away in the back seat of his truck. The wheelbarrow had to be lashed on top of the logs in the trailer. His remaining gear stowed, he drank another quart of water.

He found an area with more dead trees and marked them with surveyor's tape for his next trip. There was a game trail nearby, so he filed that information away for hunting. Downhill from the trail, he saw a pile of short pine boughs and leaves mostly covering a deer carcass. The hair on his neck bristled a little as he quickly looked around. Seeing nothing threatening, he picked up a stick and raked aside some of the branches covering the deer. He could smell the blood now and noted the opened abdominal cavity which was missing most of its organs. Intestines and stomach had been pulled out onto the ground, but not eaten. *Mountain lion*, he thought, *probably this morning*. He looked around again, then raked the branches and leaves back over the carcass, looked around one last time, and made his way back to his truck.

Driving down the mountain with the heavy load was necessarily slower than coming up. The truck proceeded at a crawl as he rounded the curves in the gravel road. Paved road finally came into view, so he stopped to check his load. Everything was secure. He would have to split some of the larger logs this week, but would wait until he had another cord. He liked to have about five cords ready for winter, though he had used less than three last year. At least one more trip up the mountain. He and his wife often joked about when they would start using fuel oil instead of enduring the annual ritual of getting firewood. It was fun, kind of, and the woods were beautiful. It was satisfying—and cheap—to provide one's own fuel. It was also hard work and maybe a little dangerous.

He got back in the driver's seat and lowered his window before starting up. He had traveled a half mile down the mountain when a Forest Service vehicle approached. Both trucks stopped.

The Forest Service officer was young and blond. A beefy arm hung out the open window.

"Been cutting that firewood or just hauling it?" he asked with a friendly smile, eyes moving quickly over Chris's truck and trailer.

"I cut this load in the woods up above Agate this morning, just a little ways back," answered Chris, jerking his head behind him. "Got the permit right here."

The officer got out of his truck and took the offered papers. He glanced at them briefly and handed them back to Chris. "Been wanting to cut some wood myself this fall but hadn't gotten around to it yet." He glanced at the snow-tinged mountains, shook his head, and laughed. "Better get after it 'less I want to be hauling logs in the snow."

Chris nodded and smiled. "Yeah, we'll get a good storm soon. Are you a new guy in the Forest Service? I know most of the fellas and don't remember seeing you before."

"Yeah, I transferred in this month. Just finding my way around and getting settled." He shook his head and chuckled. "My fiancée wanted to live in the high country, so she surely will when we say 'I do,' and meanwhile, I've got a long honey-do list. Reason I haven't put away any firewood yet." He straightened his back and looked across the valley. "Gosh, but this place is something to see."

"Yeah," said Chris, nodding, "it never gets old, least not until you have to drive in a couple of feet of snow." He got out of his truck and offered a hand to the officer. "I'm Chris Walker."

The officer shook Chris's hand and said, "Rick Doucet."

Chris nodded again in the direction from which he had come. "The ridge above Agate where I cut this load has lots of timber for the taking, and it's pretty accessible, so you might consider getting your wood up there. It's a pure stand of lodgepole, and there's plenty of stuff that's been dead for a while, some standing, some down. You could burn it this year."

"Really?" asked the officer, then chuckled. "Guess I'll need some permits. Could you show me the spot?"

"Sure. It's a pretty big area with plenty of dead wood. Plenty for both of us," said Chris with a grin. His expression sobered. "There is a lion kill up there, though. Covered up…fresh. Guess you'll be

5

okay if you're not up there too early…or too late. Better yet, don't go alone."

Rick's smile faded. "A mountain lion? You sure?"

"Well, I guess all dead deer look alike, but this one was sort of neat-killed, almost surgical. Other predators are messier, least the ones I've seen." Chris looked down and shrugged. "Don't pretend to be an expert."

"Can you show me where the kill is?" asked Rick.

Chris glanced at his watch. "Sure. Won't take long if we take your truck—leave my rig here. I'll need to call my wife, though."

"Yeah," said Rick, "I'll drive us."

"It's a mile or two from here, up above Agate, like I said before," said Chris as Rick drove back up the mountain.

"I am interested in the firewood cutting area, but I really want to know more about the lion kill, if that's what it is," said Rick as they made their way up the mountain. He paused for a few moments. "Last year, we were doing a lost-hiker search, and I found the body. Medical examiner said that the body had been out there for a while, maybe several days. We couldn't be sure if the damage to the body was done by coyotes and crows postmortem or if the cause of death was a predator kill. He wasn't old—twenty-eight—so the likelihood of the cause of death being natural wasn't very high."

Chris's forehead wrinkled. "Gosh, I'd expect a medical examiner to figure out a cause of death if it wasn't caused by a predator attack."

"You'd think," said Rick, "but the damage to the body from carrion eaters was pretty extensive…kind of grim. The ME was a new guy, a sub, not a pathologist or a professional ME. He was taking calls for the county medical examiner who was out of town. I couldn't get the substitute ME to give us a cause of death right away, but when it finally was printed, the death certificate read 'Due to advanced, apparent predator/carrion eater, damage to the body the exact cause of death cannot be determined; probably lion kill.'" Rick looked down, frowned, and said, "Damn the luck…"

"Gosh, Rick, when did all this happen?" asked Chris. He turned toward Rick. "Is there any forensic evidence left? I mean, golly, there should be a way for an expert to identify the type of wounds and all that sort of stuff." He stared at Rick for a moment, finally getting it. "Oh...you knew the guy, didn't you?"

"Yeah...my brother, Michael. He took off for a backpacking trip alone and didn't come home. We looked for him for several days. Finally found him near a county road. His body, what was left of it, was near a trailhead." Rick's voice was halting. "Not too many people were hiking that time of year, so like I said before, his body had been out there for a while."

They arrived at the woodcutting site, and Chris pointed out a spot to park the truck, near the deer carcass. They cautiously approached the cache. Rick inspected the ground around the kill. He searched the area carefully and found an area that had been disturbed, perhaps by dragging the dead animal. He followed the drag track to the trail by the boulders. He looked around and found some blood on the trail. He nodded, looking down. Following the drag line back to the cache, he pointed out some tracks near the animal.

"Lion track..." he said.

"Was he buried, Rick...your brother? Not cremated, right?"

"No, he's buried near our family home," replied Rick. "I didn't have time to get more involved in the medical examiner's evaluation because my guard unit was deployed to Southwest Asia just a few days after Micheal's burial. We hadn't even gotten the death certificate before I left. You see, we never found any of his gear: no tent, no water bottles, no backpack...no ID either. I could identify him by the tat on his shoulder." Rick looked down, shook his head, and raised his eyes to Chris. "So we don't know whether he was dragged to the spot where we found him and his campsite was somewhere else or if maybe his gear was stolen. Too many questions that we can't answer."

"Wonder if a forensic pathologist could find out anything with a reexamination? You might wanna think about it...won't bring back your brother, but it would give you an answer that's maybe better than 'probably,'" said Chris. "Messy, though, and intrusive, you know...exhumation and all. The rest of your family might not care much for the idea."

"Mom died a couple of years ago…long fight with cancer. Dad hasn't gotten over her death, and Michael dying the way he did kind of put him over the edge. Dad hasn't had much to say since we found Michael's body. My sister has never been satisfied with his cause of death…I haven't either. It seemed to be so vague…so inconclusive. After seeing this lion kill here, I'd be interested in another examination, but I wouldn't know how to get it started." Rick rolled his head, stretching his neck, gazing skyward. "We'd have to put a lot of people to a lot of trouble…I don't know…"

Chris looked at Rick for a moment, then gazed up at the mountains in the distance. He glanced back at the deer, then at Rick once more. "Maybe you have to try, Rick. I doubt that you or your family's going to rest easy until you figure this out…if it can be figured out at all. Guess you'll need an opinion by an expert who can review whatever evidence you have."

"Well," said Rick with a wry smile, "we lived in a small town, and I know all the players. I played ball with most of them or their sons. Maybe I'll be able to convince the sheriff to reopen the case. Never thought it would be worthwhile, not till I saw this kill here. This animal is covered up and, well, sort of clean. The spot where we found Michael was a mess, and so was Michael. I guess that no carcass will be 'clean' for too long, but…maybe I'm grabbing at straws…just hoping for a better answer. Fact is, Michael is dead. Maybe it's time I let it go…"

Rick's shoulders heaved with a sudden, unexpected sob.

"Rick?" said Chris. "Get a grip for a little bit here…tell me, what information do you have on this, man? Photos, lab reports, stuff like that?" asked Chris. "Maybe you and I can sift through whatever you kept and see if we have enough reasons to ask for another look?"

Rick stared hard at Chris for a moment and said, "Why're you interested in any of this?"

Chris locked his eyes on Rick's, raised his eyebrows, and said, "Don't know, Rick. Something about this just doesn't seem right. Curious, I guess. If you want me to butt out, just say the word."

Rick held his gaze for a few long seconds. His glance flicked down to the deer carcass, then back at Chris. Slowly, a mournful smile emerged.

"I'd appreciate any help you can give me, if you're up for it."

Chris nodded once and said, "I know the county ME here. He's an outdoorsman and gives seminars in wilderness medicine. I'll bet he'd be interested in reviewing your brother's case."

"Well…thanks, Chris…I don't know what to say…" said Rick.

Chris smiled at him, lightly punched him on the shoulder, and said, "Yeah, well, let's give it a try."

*****

The elderly gentleman peered slyly over his glasses at Chris. He was seated behind a massive desk covered with papers, books, a computer screen and keyboard, a badger skull, and a thick file that he was fingering absently. He had thick, shaggy gray hair that hung over his ears and onto his forehead and eyebrows that bristled over his horn-rimmed glasses. His pale gray eyes glittered.

"What are you doing here, young Chris…why is this anything to you?"

He tapped the file with his forefinger

Chris resisted the impulse to laugh and said, "Appealing to your superior knowledge, Doc."

Angus "Gus" MacDougal, MD, PhD, raised his eyebrows, his eyes boring into Chris's.

"I'm just a small-town coroner, young man, as well you know. Now give me a straight answer."

Chris's expression became serious as he replied, "Like I told you when I gave you the file, I just recently met the victim's brother. He's a Parks and Wildlife officer. He's a good guy, and he's hurting because of his brother's death. If he had some more definitive answers about the cause of his brother's death, he might be able to deal with it better. I know it's a crap shoot, Doc. Could be that whatever might be discovered will be worse than what he and the family think they know now." Chris looked down and shook his head. Raising his eyes to Dr. MacDougal, he said, "He says he wants to know more…no matter where it goes. I'd like to help him out."

Dr. MacDougal nodded slowly, glancing down at the file. He cleared his throat and pushed his glasses higher up on his nose.

"The fellow that directed the investigation, according to the documents, wasn't able to make a dispositive judgment partially because of his inexperience. He arranged for the right photographs to be taken and came to some conclusions, that, as far as they go, may turn out to be valid." He adjusted his glasses and opened the file, extracting a piece of lined paper with some pencil writing on it. "I took a few notes here. First, there isn't evidence of any blood on the ground around the body, suggesting that either the wounds on the body were not the cause of death or that if they were, the death event occurred somewhere else. Second, the tracks around the body were of different kinds: coyote (or domestic dog, maybe even fox), various birds, maybe skunk, and maybe some rodents. I don't see any tracks that appear to be cougar, but the area is so trampled that I can't rule out an earlier cougar presence either. Third, the wounds that I can see in the photographs have some of the characteristics of more than one kind of predator or carrion eater. I can't see puncture wounds on the back of the neck or claw marks on the scalp or shoulders, but again, the deterioration of the corpse is advanced enough to make judgment on those matters impossible with any degree of certainty. Fourth, lab work and drug screening of body fluids wasn't done, again, mostly because of deterioration but probably also because the cause of death was obvious."

Dr. MacDougal replaced his notes inside the file, closed the cover, and folded his hands on top of it. He adjusted his glasses again and looked at Chris.

"Cougars kill with bites to the neck, throat, or skull. Bears bite the head and neck. Wolves and coyotes disable the prey by wounding the hindquarters. X-rays and dissection of the neck and throat area would be necessary to find injuries compatible with either penetrating head trauma or spinal damage as a cause of death. Absent any typical wild predator injuries, we would have to consider so-called natural causes, most of which would be nearly impossible to identify at this late date. We have to consider a criminal cause too. There were lots of shoe prints around the body, but there is no way to tell which belonged to recovery personnel and which might belong to a perpetrator of violence."

He picked up the file and handed it to Chris.

"I would advise Officer Doucet to pursue exhumation and postmortem examination only if he is willing to accept the conclusion…or the lack thereof. I do, however, agree with both of you: no definite cause of death has been determined. I will write a letter to the county officials advising exhumation and postmortem if Officer Doucet concurs. I can perform the autopsy. I have a conference in New York at the end of the month, but that's a ways off, and I won't be gone long anyway. Just let me know one way or the other."

Dr. MacDougal rose from his chair, handed the file to Chris who had also come to his feet, smiled broadly, and said, "Let's us get together and go pop a cap at a pheasant or two sometime."

Chris nodded, took the file, and said, "I'd enjoy that."

*****

Chris's truck and utility trailer and Rick's pickup were parked near the wood-cutting area above Agate. The men had been trimming downed trees and cutting them into eight-foot lengths, the size that would fit in the truck and trailer beds. The two of them working together filled the vehicles quickly, and they were taking a water break prior to final securing of the loads and stowing of tools. Rick had been quiet and pensive. Seated on the tailgate of his truck, he took off his bill cap, wiped the sweat off his forehead, replaced the cap, and turned to Chris.

"Dr. MacDougal…uh, Gus, is quite a guy, isn't he? Doesn't pull any punches either."

"Yeah," replied Chris. "If you're not sure you want an answer, you better not ask the question."

Rick grimaced. "Right. I found that out soon enough. He comes across as a straight shooter, though. I'll be able to believe whatever answers he gets after he does the autopsy."

Chris nodded. "So you and your family have decided to go through with it?"

11

"Two out of three…one not sure: my sister and I want to know more, Dad can't make up his mind. Can't say I blame him. Just the word 'autopsy' conjures up some gruesome pictures. My fiancée doesn't think that I'll rest easy until I get some better answers. She hurts when I hurt…can't hide much from that lady." Rick smiled briefly, then his expression turned somber. "Thanks, by the way. For introducing me to Doc Gus. He inspires confidence."

Chris chuckled.

"Wait until you go hunting with him…never seen him miss and never seen him take a second shot."

"Well, I hope I have a chance to find out firsthand, one day. Guess we better finish loading up and get on home."

Rick stood up and flexed his fingers.

"Guess you'll let me know about the autopsy?" asked Chris.

"Yeah. I'll call when it's done."

Rick picked up his chain saw and put it into its carrying case. He placed the case in the back seat of his truck, gazed up at the mountains, then faced Chris.

"We can hope."

*****

Silver Lakes Daily News
Predator Kill Becomes Cold Case

Findings of an autopsy done on an exhumed body last week will result in a murder investigation. Michael Doucet, 28, had gone hiking last September and never came home. His body was found some time after he should have returned, and owing to the advanced deterioration of the corpse, the examination by the medical examiner was inconclusive: "probably lion kill." The autopsy on the exhumed body was performed by Angus MacDougal, MD, PhD, a noted forensic pathologist. His examination including X-rays disclosed evidence of a fractured skull from blunt force trauma. There were some defensive injuries of his upper extremities and a fractured hyoid bone in his neck suggesting strangulation. There were no wounds compatible with an attack by a predatory animal. Law enforcement has no suspects at this time, but results on laboratory and DNA testing will be forthcoming and may result in a break in the case.

*****

Rick had parked his pickup and trailer at the end of Chris's driveway near the woodpile. He had closed the truck door quietly and went to the back of the trailer. The tailgate served as a loading ramp and was secured with two steel pins, one on each side. Rick pulled the pins and lowered the tailgate down to the driveway. It was 6:00 a.m.

The piece of equipment perched on the trailer bed was a strange-looking thing, its purpose not likely to be obvious to anyone who did not heat his home with wood fire: it was a log splitter, gasoline powered, on wheels, and it had its own tow yoke.

Rick pulled on leather gloves. He released the tie-down straps that secured the splitter, stowed them in his truck, and walked around to the loading gate of the trailer. Climbing the gradual slope of the loading gate, he picked up the tongue of the splitter and tugged it slowly to the edge of the trailer.

A voice behind him said, "You working out for the Olympic tug-of-war or something?"

Startled, Rick looked over his shoulder, his frown relaxing when he saw Chris standing in the doorway of his house, cup of coffee in hand, dressed in sweatshirt and sweatpants.

"Come in, and I'll get you some coffee?"

Rick smiled and chuckled, shaking his head.

"I was hoping not to wake you. Guess you get up pretty early."

"Yep, don't like to miss a sunrise. Come on in."

Chris glanced at the sky for a moment and beckoned, then turned back into his mudroom.

Rick turned back to the trailer. He tugged the splitter to the break in the floor of the trailer at the hinge of the ramp. He eased the machine down the tailgate, tugging it onto the driveway, toward the woodpile, away from the back of the trailer. He raised the tailgate and secured it. Staring at Chris's house momentarily, he put his gloves in his pocket and walked to the door. He knocked on the front door once and went inside. Chris was seated at his dining room table, sipping a cup of coffee and punching keys on his laptop computer.

"Ready for a cup?" he asked.

Rick nodded assent, and Chris rose, yawning once as he walked to the kitchen counter nearby and poured coffee into a large plain white mug. He put the mug on the table and said, "Cream and sugar if you want it."

Rick took off his hat and sat down and picked up the mug.

"Nope, black is good. Thanks for letting me use the splitter. Works like a charm. I topped off fuel and crankcase oil. Tire pressures are good."

"Anytime," said Chris. "Not sure why I bought the darn thing. No more than I use it, it'd be cheaper to rent one."

They sat in silence for a few minutes, sipping their coffee.

"Got a call from the sheriff back home…Silver Lakes. He's been working on my brother's case." Rick paused, swallowed some coffee and said, "He's made an arrest. Got a CODIS match last week on DNA recovered from Michael's body…some tissue under his fingernails, some blood on the knuckles of his right hand…looks like Michael got in at least one lick. Seems the suspect has been a petty thief and sort of a no-account thug…he's hung around our town for years. Did some time for burglary. Long rap sheet. Couple of assault and battery charges and some domestic violence. Sheriff recovered Michael's backpack at this guy's home. Some blood on a tire iron in his car matched Michael's. Oughta be a slam dunk from here." Rick looked into his coffee mug. "Guess it's kind of over…"

Chris stared at him and said, "Well, yeah, as much as these things are ever over…Michael has had justice, finally. Still, what you know now will take some getting used to."

"I thought I was used to Michael being gone…guess I'll have to do it all over again. And that'll have to wait 'til after the trial and sentencing and then all of the appeals. It'll be awhile, so I'll need to change my attitude." Rick looked into his coffee cup again. "I tell myself to let it go, but then I feel like it wouldn't be fair to Michael if I did…kind of copping out."

"Wasn't a cop-out to ask Doc Gus to look into Michael's case, was it?" asked Chris with a raised eyebrow. "Michael is gone, Rick. You'll want to remember the best and put the bad parts…those things you can't do anything about anyway, put those sad parts away." Chris paused. "Easier said than done, I know. It'll take time."

Chris stopped talking. He knew he was rambling.

"Right," said Rick, taking a swallow of coffee and putting the cup down on the table. "Guess I'll figure out a way to deal with it." He glanced at Chris, then looked out the window at the mountains. "Thanks for your help with this, Chris. Be seeing you."

He put on his hat, stood, and walked out the door, closing it quietly behind him.

*****

Three men walked slowly across the frosty field that was covered with remnants of cornstalks. The sky was overcast, and the early morning air was calm and chilly. The field had been picked in September, and enough corn lay on the ground to attract pheasant. Each man carried a shotgun. A German shorthaired pointer roamed back and forth ahead of the men, nose to the ground, stopping ever so often to examine clumps of cornstalk. Dr. Angus MacDougal was in the center, a little ahead of the other two men. Chris was on his right, Rick on his left, each about fifty feet away.

They approached a hedgerow which extended obliquely across the field, nearer to Rick than to Chris. The pointer became interested in the hedge near Gus.

"May be something in there," he said.

The dog came to a point, and the hunters readied their weapons, thumbing safeties as they advanced closer to the hedge. When he was about twenty feet away from the pointing dog, Gus stopped, turned a little to his right, and glanced left and right.

"Ready?" he said in a low voice.

"Yep," said Rick.

"Go for it," murmured Chris.

Gus crept forward a few more feet, stopped, shouldered his shotgun, and stomped his right boot on the ground as he yelled, "Get up!"

In a surprisingly loud flutter of wings, two pheasants rose from the hedgerow, one flying straight away from the hunters, one flying to the right. The shotgun blasts were nearly simultaneous, Gus's a fraction earlier than Chris's. Both roosters fell. The dog broke point, sat, and looked up at Gus. Gus looked down at the dog, waited a moment, and said, "Go get 'em, girl!"

The dog ran forward and hopped over the hedge. She spotted the near rooster and bore down on him in seconds. Picking up the pheasant, she ran back to Gus, dropping the bird at his feet. She immediately sat and looked up at her owner who pointed toward the other downed pheasant and said, "Get that dead bird, Rusty!"

The dog turned and again ran back to the hedgerow, easily vaulting the three-foot-high shrub. She scanned left and right, then ran toward the remaining bird. Returning with the rooster, she again put it down before her owner and sat, eyes locked on Gus's face.

Gus said, "Good dog!" as he got a scrap of jerky out of his pocket and fed it to her. She swallowed the tidbit and stared expectantly at her owner's face.

"That's enough for now, pup," said Angus, smiling down at the dog, briefly patting the dog's head. Rick and Chris had joined Gus, their over/under shotguns opened at the breeches.

"Good shooting, Doc," said Rick. "Guess that gives us our limits."

Earlier, Rick had shot one bird, Chris one, and Gus two.

"Yes indeed. Time to go home," said Gus with a broad smile, scratching the dog's neck. The pointer smiled and nudged her owner's knee.

They unloaded their shotguns and picked up the pheasants. Hanging the opened weapons over their shoulders, they walked back across the field toward their trucks which were parked along the farm road a half mile away. Gus looked over at Rick and said,

"Your hometown sheriff did some good investigative work on your brother's case."

"Yes, he did, Dr. Gus. But the evidence that your postmortem came up with gave him everything he needed to locate the perp," said Rick, looking at the ground, watching his steps on the uneven ground. "Gave us an idea what happened too." He shook his head. "Hard to believe that theft is reason enough to kill a man."

"Uh-huh," said Gus. "Hard to figure out why people do some of the things they do."

"Well," said Chris, glancing at Rick, "now that the trial and sentencing are over, you'll be able to think about the other important things in your life, like when're you going to marry that girl?"

"Yeah," said Rick with a broad, effortless smile, "things like that. I figure it'll be soon…before Easter I bet."

Two Bucks

He was walking quietly through the open meadow paralleling the woods in the dim light of the early morning. The animal that he was stalking was hidden, back in the trees. It snorted occasionally and rustled in the undergrowth every few steps. Then it would pause, watchful, and move on again, ghostly, with scarcely any sound. He was tense. He gripped his rifle tightly, puffing clouds of vapor as he breathed the frigid air. He followed the edge of the timber, placing his feet carefully but finally broke the silence when he stepped on a fallen branch, which snapped in two with a loud crack. The animal snorted, loudly this time, and bolted, breaking free of the wood, well ahead of the hunter, galloping into the meadow, crunching the frozen ground as it ran, quartering away from the man, who never got a good look at his prey.

*****

Chris awakened from the dream in a startle. He sat up in bed and turned toward his alarm clock. It was 5:00 a.m. The alarm had not sounded. He toggled the alarm button off.

He crept quietly downstairs after closing the bedroom door behind him. Pulling on a sweater that was hanging on a chair back at the bottom of the stairs, he started the coffeepot and opened the shades covering the windows that faced south.

Orion appeared high in the clear sky on this first day of deer hunting season, the middle of October. He gazed at the constellation for a long moment, then turned to the kitchen, poured some black coffee, and prepared his breakfast, along with an extra plate of eggs and bacon for his wife to reheat later.

His hunting clothes were laid out in his den as were his daypack and accessories. Finishing his breakfast, he checked the weather on his computer and, satisfied with the report, put his utensils in the kitchen sink and went into the downstairs bathroom to shower and shave.

He dressed in layers: long silk underwear, camouflage pants, and pullover shirt. Wool socks and wool sweater came next. His outer wear lay in a neatly arranged pile by the door. The daypack, blaze orange in color, had already been packed, but Chris removed the contents once again, consulted a checklist retrieved from one of the pockets in the pack, and replaced everything, adding three plastic bottles of water and an apple. He got his rifle and ammunition pouch out of the gun safe and found his orange bill cap and vest along with his camouflage pattern hooded jacket hanging in the mudroom closet. He finished putting on his hunting clothes, put his license and ID in his zippered jacket pocket, and strapped a battery-operated headlamp about the crown of his cap. Binocular strap around his neck and rifle slung over his right shoulder, he went out of west door of his house and turned north, threading his way through the sagebrush, seeing the evanescent fog of his breath in the cold of the predawn. Polaris winked high in the sky ahead, and the great black masses of mountains appeared as irregular, featureless silhouettes on the eastern and the western sides of the valley.

*****

He walked north for a half mile, then turned east into a broad-mouthed wash that cut through the rocks near the border into

National Forest. Another half mile into the wash, gradually increasing in altitude, he found the surveyor's tape markers that he had placed some days past, tied to a low tree limb and to a serviceberry bush. This area was crisscrossed with game trails which he had been scouting for the past two weeks. He had found plenty of evidence of deer, lots of track and scat. He climbed the north-facing bank some forty or fifty feet and located the large partially buried boulder situated between a piñon pine and a mountain mahogany, the branches of each providing some cover but not much obstruction to his view of the wash.

The alpenglow on the mountaintops appeared as the sun rose and reflected luminously on the western peaks as Chris watched from the shadows. His several thin layers of clothing felt snug and warm in the near-freezing air. The sky was mostly clear with a few high cirrus clouds, lit pink just now. Things would warm up in a little while.

Chris scanned the wash below and the bank across from his position continuously. He had seen a number of does, some with fawns. One spike buck and a little fork buck had come down the bank across from him. He had evaluated each animal and rejected both: too young, too small. A little too dark for a sure shot anyway.

He was scanning the opposite bank with his binoculars, once again in the gradually brighter light, when he heard gunfire coming from the east, the sharp staccato crack of a high-velocity firearm. Three shots, two close together, the third following a second or two later...had to be an autoloader or more than one rifle...he guessed about a half mile away, owing mainly to the length of the wash and the surrounding terrain. He wondered if it was a kill or a miss. Hunters who didn't live close by approached this area in their vehicles from the county road to the east, parking their trucks and walking a mile or so into the mountainous terrain, slightly downhill, in search of a good place to sit and wait for deer to wander by or to stalk them. He hoped that the successful hunter would be laboriously hauling his kill uphill to his truck since there was no public access to this terrain from the west. A few local hunters would know private landowners who might let them cross their properties to access the higher ground from the west. This was the more desirable approach because of the relative ease of dragging a deer carcass downhill. Most of the landowners that Chris knew, however, didn't want any hunting near their homes, so No Trespassing signs were common along the county roads. The likely outcome of the gunfire would therefore not be something that would affect Chris's stand, so he continued scanning the target area that he had selected, giving some attention to the right side of wash area since there was an outside chance that a deer spooked by the gunfire would come from the east.

A few minutes went by, and then a three-point mule deer buck trotted down the sandy wash from the east. He paused momentarily, then turned up the far bank. His antlers were symmetrical and shiny.

The animal stopped, looked over his shoulder, then gazed at the terrain to the south. He looked straight at Chris, stared for a moment at the immobile figure which he couldn't identify, then continued looking around. He raised his head and sniffed the air. Chris was downwind, his scent not accessible to the animal's acute sense of smell. Chris raised his binoculars slowly and found the buck in the Nikons. He was a healthy-appearing big-bodied animal with an unblemished coat on the visible side. The buck grazed on a patch of grass as Chris tucked his binoculars inside his coat and raised his rifle. He thumbed the safety off and peered through the scope, centering the crosshairs just behind the buck's shoulder. He took a deep breath, partially let it out, concentrated on his target, and slowly squeezed the trigger. He felt the butt plate hammer his shoulder as the muzzle rose a little, rocking his slight body backward a tad. He then reacquired his target and watched the downed animal through his scope as he worked the bolt for a follow-up shot if he needed it. Ten or fifteen seconds passed, and the buck remained still.

Chris thumbed the rifle's safety to the safe position, picked up the expended cartridge case, and dropped it in his pocket as he came to his feet, holding the rifle in both hands, watching the deer continuously. He picked his way downhill to the floor of the wash, then up the north side to the animal. The buck had crumpled to his knees and fallen upslope.

Chris noted the wound behind the shoulder, maybe a little high, and the superficial wound on a ham. The earlier gunfire had not been entirely in vain. He approached the deer from his flank and poked him gently in the back with his riffle barrel...no response. Chris walked around the animal uphill and again poked the deer, this time in his neck. Confirming that the buck was dead, Chris slung his rifle and knelt beside his head. He sensed motion to his left as he heard a voice saying, "What'cha doin' to my buck?"

Two men were walking up the slope toward him, both dressed in hunter's camo with the requisite blaze-orange caps and vests. The man in front looked to be in his forties, stocky, medium height, though taller than Chris, and red-faced. He stared at Chris through squinted eyes—he had an annoyed expression on his face, a tight-lipped grimace, and furrowed brow. He had a feed store logo embroidered on his orange bill cap. The other man was an older teen, tall, slim, and light on his feet. He appeared to be surprised and a little hesitant; he looked uncomfortable. Both carried AR-style rifles and each held his rifle in both hands, muzzles pointed downward. Neither man carried a pack.

Chris rose slowly, frowned a little, and meeting the older man's glare, said, "If I hadn't brought him down, he'd be in the next county by now. I shot this deer in the heart, stone dead. Guess he's my deer."

He stood his rifle on the ground, butt first, holding it by the barrel.

The older man's eyes glinted. They flickered down and left, rose to glare at Chris, and said, "I don't see it that way. I winged him. You just finished him off."

He raised the muzzle of his rifle just a little.

Chris looked him in the eye for a long moment, then at the younger man who met his gaze momentarily and looked down, lowering his gun barrel fractionally.

Chris glanced at the older man again briefly, then clenched his jaw in a sardonic grin, slung his rifle on his right shoulder and turned away from them toward the wash. He walked down the slope to the bottom of the wash and continued to the west, rounding the slight bend in the trail a few minutes later, out of sight of the two men. He heard a voice and the brief bark of a mirthless laugh behind him as he walked. He took a deep breath, pursed his lips, and shook his head slightly, once, and continued walking, more to the south side of the wash, in the shadows of the scattered fir trees along the side of the trail.

He stopped a few minutes later and sat down on a rock. Plucking a fresh cartridge from a pouch on his belt, he removed the magazine from his rifle, pushed the cartridge into the magazine, and reinserted it into the bottom of the receiver. He retrieved the spent cartridge case from his pocket, kicked a shallow divot in the sandy floor of the wash with his heel, dropped the cartridge case in, and kicked sand over the hole. Pulling a water bottle from one of the mesh pockets on his pack, he took a long swallow. Replacing the water bottle, he raised his binoculars to scan the wash and the hillside to the north. He completed his scan, then did it again. Finding nothing of interest, he rose and began walking slowly in the patchy shade, continuing west toward the mouth of the wash.

He walked another five minutes or so, stopping occasionally to scan the area ahead with his binoculars. He stopped when he perceived motion to his right, maybe a hundred yards ahead...no, a hundred twenty-five. Two does came out of the piñon high on the bank to his right and trotted obliquely down the slope away from him toward the opposite bank. Chris continued to watch the area from which the does had come. A few seconds passed and a large buck crept cautiously into view between two piñon pines. His head, neck, and left foreleg were visible, the remainder of his body hidden behind a tree branch. He had nicely symmetrical antlers with a broad basket and four points plus a brow tine on each side. His coat, what Chris could see of it, was slick appearing and shiny. He was thick about the neck and body and had a grizzled muzzle.

Chris slowly squatted down to a seated position in the dirt, in the shadow of a ponderosa, knees high, raising his rifle and balancing it atop the triangle of two knees, elbow on each, and a shoulder, leaning into the anticipated shot, sighting through the scope, placing the crosshairs as far to the rear of the animal's visible neck as possible and waited, breathing slowly, pulse up a little, concentrating on the deer. No clear shot...yet.

The deer's head went down and out of sight, and Chris continued to stare at the general area. The field of view of the rifle scope included the piñon pine on either side of where the buck had first appeared, and Chris moved the rifle side to side, slowly, in search of the hidden animal. The anticipation of the remarkably slow passage of what was probably only a few seconds ended with the reappearance of the buck a little uphill of the two piñon pines and standing in the open. He'd go 200, maybe 225 pounds. He was eating from a patch of grass he had found in the scree of the bank, occasionally raising his head, looking around, then putting his head down, and continuing to graze.

Chris squirmed a little, repositioning himself slightly, thumbed the safety off, put the crosshairs on the area behind the deer's shoulder, controlled his breathing, and squeezed off the shot. He controlled the barrel rise and reacquired the animal which had jumped a little, taken a few steps, then fallen. Chris watched him, where he lay motionless, for a few seconds. He worked the bolt, thumbed the safety, and picked up the spent cartridge case, keeping the deer in sight. He came to his feet and made his way across the wash and up the bank to the deer, keeping his eyes on the downed animal. The deer was in a near-squatted position, leaning into a steep spot in the bank. Chris poked him in the hindquarter with his gun barrel, walked uphill around the animal, and poked his shoulder. No response. Chris looked around, a 360-degree survey. He put his rifle down on the ground and took off his pack and his jacket, donning again the orange vest. The wound in the animal's chest was behind the shoulder, about right…easy shot. He knelt, stroked the hair on the buck's neck, whispered something, and came to his feet. He grasped an antler and pulled the deer over, downhill, looking for the exit wound. He found it and continued to drag the deer so that his head was downslope. No slug recovery today. He got his license and a pen from the jacket pocket. He tore off the carcass tag, marked it properly, signed it, and tied it to the animal with a piece of string poked through a hole stabbed through an ear.

First reloading his rifle and rechecking the safety, he retrieved the several items from his pack needed to field-dress the deer and completed the task quickly, salvaging heart and liver, each in its separate plastic bag. After disposing of his plastic gloves in another bag, he returned all his gear and bags to the pack and wiped his brow with a shirtsleeve. Getting warmer. He tied his thick jacket to the top of his backpack and drank some water. Putting on his pack, he cross-chest slung his rifle. A length of a half-inch braided rope from his pack tied around the buck's antlers at their bases made a simple towing harness. The gut pile remained. Thanks to the birds and coyotes, it would be gone by sunset.

He looked around one last time and began tugging the carcass down the slope at an angle to the floor of the wash. The floor was slightly downhill, making easier the task of dragging his deer through the sand. In a half hour, he was located at the mouth of the wash, the higher terrain behind him smoothly blending into the valley ahead. What used to be a Forest Service road, a two-track, crossed private property to the maintained county road visible about three hundred yards to the west. High mountains were about ten miles away, across the broad valley. The National Forest boundary marker was just ahead.

Chris stopped, took off his harness, rifle, and pack, and sat down on a rock. He rooted around in his pack and came up with a water bottle and the apple. He took off his cap and wiped his forehead with his shirtsleeve, then downed half of the quart bottle of water in one draught and was well into the apple when he heard voices behind him, back to the east. He looked over his shoulder and saw two men dragging a deer along the wash, following his recent track. The older red-faced man tugged on an antler in his left hand and the taller younger man grasped the other antler with his right. They were sweaty and stumbling in the soft sand. Chris wondered why they were coming this way—their vehicle must be in the opposite direction. They finally saw Chris seated on the rock and stopped, maybe thirty feet away, staring at him, the older man turning to his companion and murmuring something.

Chris stood, returned the water bottle and the remains of the apple to his pack, and walked toward the two men, noticing that the animal had not been field-dressed and that a carcass tag was not visible. The men looked tired.

"That deer would be easier to drag if you'd gut it first," he said.

The older man puffed, "We left our knives in our truck... What's it to you anyway?"

"It's a long way to drag the animal back to your truck," replied Chris, "so you better lighten the load. Better put a carcass tag on him, too. Game warden takes a dim view of an unmarked carcass. I can loan you a knife."

"No," the older man responded, "we'll just haul the deer down to that road and hitch a ride back to our truck. Gut him later."

"You're about to trespass on a patch of private property," said Chris, waving a hand toward the National Forest boundary marker. "Can't get the deer out this way without permission from the landowner."

The older man sneered. "I guess you have permission?"

"Don't need permission," said Chris with a wry smile, "It's my land."

The younger man quickly looked away with a flicker of a smile. The older man's shoulders sagged. He sat down in the dirt and pulled a large blue kerchief from a pocket. He used it to mop his face as he gazed tight-jawed at the ground. Chris stared at them briefly and glanced toward the county road. He turned back toward the younger man who met his stare with a steady gaze. Chris turned back toward the mountains across the valley for a moment longer and sighed deeply. The skin around his eyes crinkled as he quickly glanced at the younger man again. He turned to his pack, fished out a knife, a six-inch drop-point skinner in its sheath, a little blood on the blade and the handle, and a bottle of water and tossed both on the sandy ground in front of the younger man. He put on his pack, shouldered his rifle, and slung the towing harness across his chest. Turning to the men, he said, "Gut the deer and drag him down to the road. I'll be back in about an hour with my truck. I can take one of you to get your vehicle."

He turned away and began dragging his deer along the two-track, west toward the county road.

The younger man laid his rifle on the ground. Stripping off his jacket, he picked up the knife. He removed the knife from its sheath, sticking the sheath in his pocket, then cautiously tested the knife edge with his thumb. Good-lookin' knife.

"That was a surprise," he said. "Nice guy."

The older man glowered and shook his head slightly. He opened his mouth to speak, thought better of it, and looked down at the ground.

"Sharp knife, Dad," said the younger man, glancing quickly at his father. "Do you want to do this or do you want me to?"

He handed the bottle of water to the older man.

The older man nodded toward his son. "Go ahead, Caleb—if you think you can."

He sat down on a nearby rock and opened the bottle of water. He took a long swallow, then another one. Taking off his hat, he wiped his brow with his shirtsleeve.

Caleb rolled up his sleeves. "Yessir, I can do it…been cleaning whitetails for a couple of years now. After Mom and I moved to Llano. Guess this guy will be about the same."

His father raised his eyebrows, pursed his lips, and nodded. "Some big deer around Llano, I've heard. I knew you'd done some hunting…didn't know how much, I guess. Never had time to get down there."

"Uncle John helped me pick out a rifle and has been taking me deer hunting every year. He let me tag along with him and his boys, starting a few years back. They're all good shots. Good teachers too… they taught me how."

"Too bad John's such a prick whenever I see him. Guess I couldn't expect much else after me and your mom split up." He looked up at his son, seeing the frown and tensed jaw. "Anyway, there wasn't much time for us to talk after I picked you up from the airport yesterday," said his father. "Not much time to get used to the altitude either. I'm draggin' ass. We're a long way from Fort Worth," he added.

"Yessir. Must have been a tough drive. We need to figure out where to get the deer butchered. Do you know of anybody around here that does that?" asked Caleb.

"Yeah, I got a couple of phone numbers, if we can find some-body willing to do it…kind of short notice. We'll call 'em when we get back to the motel," replied his father. "Otherwise, we'll have to do it ourselves."

"Dad, can you come hold a leg for me?" asked Caleb as he finished opening the buck's abdomen.

*****

The two men were sitting under a weathered elm tree beside the county road. The tree had a few remaining yellow-brown leaves, and the field-dressed buck lay nearby in the partial shade. Chris came to a stop beside them in his pickup truck, an older model four-door with an extended bed and snow tires. It had a beat-up bumper with an enclosed winch. Spattered mud decorated the doors and fenders.

He spoke through the open window. "One of you ought to stay with the deer. Who wants to ride?"

The younger man came to his feet, nodded toward his father, and approached the truck. He carried his rifle and his jacket.

"Rifle okay in the back seat?" he asked.

"Sure," Chris said. "Make sure the chamber is empty and put the magazine in your pocket. Fish and Wildlife people, y'know."

When the young man had gotten into the truck, Chris said, "Your vehicle's on County Road 226, right? Uh, got your keys?"

The young man nodded and waved to his father as they drove away.

"My name is Chris Walker," said Chris. "What's yours?"

"Caleb McKewen," said the young man. "I appreciate the ride."

"Uh-huh. You'll want to get that deer hung, out of the sun, soon as you can."

Caleb nodded, staring straight ahead. "That's a neat little knife you loaned us. Sharp too. Never gutted a mulie before. They're bigger than the whitetails we have in Texas. That knife is kinda plain...I mean, it doesn't have any markings or...anything. Pretty scales, too...looks to be walnut. Is it custom made?"

"Yeah," said Chris. "I make 'em out of old table saw blades. Keeps me busy on those snowy days. Kinda fun."

Caleb raised his eyebrows and looked at Chris. He was quiet for a few moments. "Sorry, my dad was so grouchy…felt bad about that. He's always been a grouchy kind of guy…guess that's why him and Mom aren't married anymore."

Chris thought for a moment, looking straight ahead at the gravel road. "Well, maybe he'll mellow out one of these days." He glanced at Caleb briefly, pursing his lips. "Even if he doesn't, he's still your dad."

Caleb stared at him for a moment, then looked forward and nodded to himself.

"Good shooting on the deer." He looked over his shoulder at the weapon lying on the back seat beside his own. "Good-lookin' rifle, too. What caliber?" asked Caleb.

"It's a .280 Remington," replied Chris. "If I had it to do over again it would have been a .270…easier to get ammo. The ballistics are close. The .280 is a little faster and shoots a little flatter, depending on the round…they all shoot where you point 'em, though. Do you like your AR?"

"It's my Dad's. He likes the semiauto and the cheap ammo," said Caleb. "I shoot an aught-six when we hunt whitetails in Llano…it's an old Winchester model 70…Bushnell scope…works pretty good. Dad has the two ARs, so he brought them along. Saved me having to carry my rifle on the plane."

"Aught-six is a good round. Been more deer killed with that one and .30-30 than you can shake a stick at. The heavier loads are good for elk, too. You could do worse," said Chris. "I can't imagine using an autoloader for deer. Good solution for a nonproblem. One shot is all you need, most of the time." He grinned and glanced at Caleb. "'Less what your shootin' at can fight back. Anyway, a bolt gun will give you another shot if you need it." He shrugged and shifted his hands on the steering wheel. "Different strokes, I guess."

Chris was driving uphill on the washboard road when a broad curve exposed a shallow valley with a mountainous panorama further to the east, remnants of fall color change streaking the evergreen hillsides with orange and gold, the sun well above the horizon in an incredibly blue sky. The most distant mountains appeared in a series of silhouettes, fading in a gauzy mist near the horizon.

"Somethin' to see, isn't it?" he said, slowing down a little.

"Yessir. It is. Nothing like this in Texas," said Caleb. "Least not this high up."

"Yeah," said Chris, grinning. "It's pretty special. Guess that's why folks live here." He stopped the truck and pointed to some trees downhill to the east. "There's a creek down there by those cotton-woods, and two to three game trails lead down to it. There's been some nice bucks in there, last couple of years. If you and your dad have another tag between you, you might go down there one morning and see if you can find one." He put the truck in gear and proceeded along the gravel road. "That your truck ahead?"

Chris pointed at the late-model pickup truck parked alongside the road.

"Yessir."

The truck came to a stop, and Caleb got the ignition key out of his pants pocket. He got out, opened the rear door to get his rifle, and closed both doors. He looked in the open window and, finding the knife in his hip pocket, said, "Thanks again for the ride. Here's your knife."

Chris gazed at the mountains, thought for a moment, and turned back to the young man. "Why don't you keep it, Caleb? It'll remind you of the first mulie you field-dressed. Besides, you might need it for another one, next day or two."

He smiled at the young man and nodded once, then he put his truck in gear and drove away.

*****

Caleb and his father drove down the long grade toward the city soon after daylight, the high mountain air cool and crisp. The light was bright on the rocks, the trees, and the fields of asters and grass, all etched with the sharpness and clarity of the early morning.

"Can you get dry ice for the meat on the way to Fort Worth?" asked Caleb.

"There's places in Dumas and Amarillo that I've used before. No matter. The trip is short enough that I can use a couple of bags of cube ice to get home…guess I'll be there before midnight, if some jerk doesn't try to run over me on the highway," replied his dad, tight-lipped and pugnacious at the imagined event.

He took a deep breath, glanced at his son, and said, "I can send your backstrap steaks in one of the mailing coolers that I have at home. UPS says that they can set it on your doorstep a few hours after they put it on the plane, if you believe 'em." He looked over at his son again and paused, caught in a moment of indecision, looked back at the highway. "Maybe I can drive down to Llano sometime later on this month and drop off the rest of your deer meat. You and your mom can find room for it in a freezer…I guess…" He coughed and cleared his throat. "That sure was a good shot on that six point that you got. Dropped him in his tracks. Good thing the guy that did the processing could take care of both deer."

"Yessir, a pretty lucky shot," said Caleb. "Hope you can get down to Llano…It'd be good to see you again, Dad. We'll go get a burger or something. Maybe you could bring my antlers…that three- by-three rack would look good on the wall at home…if Mom can put up with it." He looked out the window for a moment. "It was mighty nice of Chris to tell us about that creek bed. Cool guy."

"Yeah," said his father as they turned in to the departure lanes at the airport. He nodded and coughed again. "Chris is a good man… better than…well…he's a good man." He cleared his throat. "Far as getting to Llano goes, we'll see…yeah, we'll see."

Getting Caught

The dry fly came to rest on the water just downstream of a rock in the quiet eddy there. It swayed gently in the glittering water for a moment until a swirl from beneath roiled the surface, and the brown trout broke free, taking the fly in its boney lips, completely clearing the surface of the river before crashing, side first, back into the water. The fly line went taut, and Chris raised the tip of his rod, maintaining control over the fish and directing its frantic dash toward the deeper water, clear of rocks, near the middle of the river. He stripped off some line from the reel with his left hand, letting the trout run a little, managing tension on the line by pressing it against the rod with his right forefinger. The fish streamed to the left, glistening just beneath the surface, and rose again, not as high this time, and sped back to the right as soon as it fell back into the water. Chris kept the rod tip high and rotated his wrist side to side, maintaining control of the fish. Alternating pulling in on the line in excess of releasing, it gradually brought the trout closer. Finally, after ten or fifteen minutes, the trout was thrashing about at his knees. Christ extended the short-handled net on its elastic tether and scooped up the tiring fish. About eighteen inches… nice fish…'bout right for dinner.

Chris had caught and released several trout over the past couple of hours and had kept only one, a little smaller than the one in his net. He had parked his truck downstream a half a mile or so and slowly waded the river upstream, stopping to cast his fly ever so often when he found a spot that looked promising.

He tucked the rod beneath his right arm, extracted a plastic bag from the musette bag hanging beneath his left arm, and deposited the trout in the bag after removing the fly from its mouth. This fish joined the one caught earlier in the musette bag.

Chris retrieved his fly line, which was floating a good ways downstream by now, snugly winding it onto the reel. Enough fishing for this morning. Besides, a little breeze was coming up out of the north, not good for casting a fly line. He was conscious of the cold river water about his lower legs and knees, its gentle but relentless tugging at him. He wore short pants and felt-soled boots over neoprene socks instead of waders, safer for walking on the slick rocks in the river, lighter, and easier to stow in his truck. Colder, though, in the fall and winter days. Fly-fishing the river was fun this time of year because the tourists had mostly gone home and his only competition was from local fishermen and from hunters to wanted a break from stalking deer or elk or bighorn sheep. His big-game hunting season was over with the taking of a nice buck last week, so putting some fish on the table and in the freezer was his next winter preparation activity.

There was snow visible on the high mountains some miles to the west, but none had accumulated in the valley. There was a thin rime of ice at the river edge earlier this morning, but it was gone now since the air had warmed. The ground rose gradually from the river on the west side, but rose more steeply to the east, gaining forty or fifty feet before reaching the county road that ran along the river. East of the road, the terrain continued to rise sharply into the low mountains defining the eastern border of the wide valley.

The county road was gravel and built on an old railroad bed. It was slightly serpentine, following the meandering course of the river.

There were wider areas of the road where parking was safe and other areas that were so narrow that only one vehicle at a time could pass, the width of the road determined by some gigantic boulders that were much too large to easily move. Some piñon pine and a variety of bushes and sagebrush grew alongside the road and on the banks of the river and above the road. The cottonwoods and elms were near the end of their color change, and fallen yellow leaves lined the river edges. Ospreys and an occasional bald eagle hunted the river, and their voluminous nests could be found in the tops of some of the trees, usually old, dead ponderosas or Douglas firs rising high above the water line. There were mountain lions in the area, and bighorn sheep and elk grazed the higher terrain. Mule deer were plentiful, and all of these animals came down from the higher hills and meadows to drink from the river.

Chris made his way to the shore and put down his gear. He took the fish out of his bag and cleaned them in the river, tossing the entrails far up on the bank—crow food. He wrapped the fish in the plastic bags again and replaced them in the musette bag.

He disassembled his fly rod and arranged his gear for the climb up the bank to the road. He planned to walk back to his truck on the road rather than along the river edge: easier, faster, and safer. The sound of the river was surprisingly loud as he made his way up the trail that zigzagged up the bank through the bushes and trees.

He was halfway up the bank when he glanced to the south through a clear spot in the bushes and noticed a man sitting on top of a large rock by the road, maybe fifty yards away. The rock rose maybe ten or fifteen feet above the road bed, and the man was facing south, motionless. Chris stood still, eyes scanning right and left. He thought for a few moments, glanced back to the north, and finally, found another man sitting on top of a high rock, gazing north. Strange. He would have expected those visitors who came to contemplate nature to gaze at the mountains or at the river, not down the road. He stood still for a moment, then continued climbing the bank.

When the road bed was at eye level, Chris saw two vehicles parked on the far side of the road, maybe thirty feet away. He was looking at the two trucks through some grass and boulder raspberry bushes on the river side of the road, so he was not visible to the men working between the trucks. The truck facing north was a refrigerator van that had a food delivery service logo decorating the side of the cargo box. Backed up behind it was a full-sized long-bed pickup truck with a high camper shell, the tailgates open. Two men were dragging something in a black plastic bag out of the back of the pickup. Chris finally identified it when the seven-by seven antlered elk head emerged: this was a caped trophy elk. The two men laboriously moved the head to the door of the van and disappeared inside with their load. They emerged a few moments later and returned to the pickup. One of the men paused, took off his hat, and wiped his brow with his shirtsleeve. He was medium height with dark hair and a full bushy mustache. He replaced his hat and turned toward the pickup truck. Chris watched as the two men transferred another elk head, two bighorn sheep heads, both full recurves, three mule deer heads, and two unidentifiable black plastic bags which were bulky and apparently heavy. He took the smartphone out of his pocket and took some pictures of the scene, capturing some of the animal parts, but not much detail of the two men, dressed as they were in dark monotones and black wool watch caps. He checked the cell tower reception symbol on the phone and found "no service." The irregular terrain here was broken with mountains and canyons, so much of the county had no cell phone service.

Quietly retreating down the trail back to the riverbank, he hurried to the south toward his truck. He needed to cover the distance quickly but was slowed down by the terrain along the riverbank. There were areas where the bank was steep, others where there were large boulders impeding his progress. He scanned the bank to his left, looking for the man sitting on the rock, but saw no one. The three quarter-mile scamper seemed to take forever, but finally, he trotted up the trail to the road bed where his truck was parked.

He quickly off-loaded his gear, changed his boots, and started the truck. He turned the truck around and hurried along the gravel road to the south. The terrain opened up to a wider, flatter part of the valley, and Chris turned on his mobile phone. Cell service available.

He slowed down, cruised to the side of the road, and stopped, deep in thought. The transfer and transport of animal parts were not in themselves illegal. There could be a reasonable explanation for the multiple trophy heads being in one place at the same time. The refrigerator truck could belong to a taxidermist or perhaps a hunting club. The presence of two lookouts, if that is what they were, was suspicious, however, and if the situation had a legitimate explanation, then a police stop would cost the truck operators nothing but a little time. He keyed in 911 and explained what he had seen to the sheriff office dispatcher, describing the logo on the side of the refrigerator truck. The pickup truck was not especially notable, but he gave a brief description of that vehicle too. The dispatcher explained to Chris that both Sheriff's Office and the Fish and Game Department would be contacting him. Chris acknowledged and hung up. He let out a deep breath that he didn't know he was holding, checked his mirrors, and drove home.

*****

The wheelbarrow was piled high with split firewood. Chris lifted the handles and forced the wheelbarrow up the slight incline some thirty feet to the wall of his house nearest to his front door. He wore an old leather jacket, bill cap, some gloves, and a pair of steel-toed boots peeked out from under his camo pants legs. There was a mudroom behind the entry door to his house, an atrium commonly found in the high country used for muddy boots, jackets, and gloves and as much firewood as the room could hold during the winter. The eaves of his home near the front door extended two feet over the cement porch and provided some protection from snow. This was where Chris had more firewood stored, well away from the huge pile of split and blocked logs located well away from the house at the end of his driveway. He was nearly finished stacking the wood when he noticed the white pickup truck coming up his long driveway. There was some sort of logo painted on the door and a white-and-blue light bar over the cab. The truck was fitted with studded snow tires, and a robust-appearing wench was bolted to the massive aftermarket front bumper that had a headlight and grill- protecting steel frame welded on. The truck came to a stop near his woodpile, and a stocky man wearing a tan and green National Forest Service uniform got out. Lyle Thibodeaux was about 5'11" and weighed a good 220 pounds. He had wide shoulders, a thick neck, and muscular arms, and was remarkably light on his feet, all evidence of his college athletic career.

He had blond hair clipped close to his skull and pale blue eyes. His ruddy/tanned complexion had the white raccoon eyes caused by the aviator-style sunglasses that he had just removed and hung by an earpiece from his shirt pocket. A broad smile transformed a homely face into one that was pleasant and engaging. He leaned against his truck door, his left forearm resting on the holstered Springfield .45 ACP on his duty belt. The belt was festooned with gear: a radio, a Taser, spare magazines, handcuffs.

"How's it goin', Chris?" he said.

Chris approached and took off his right glove. He offered his hand as he neared the other man.

"Doin' fine, Lyle. You?"

"Oh, life is good, I reckon. Every day on the sunny side of the dirt is a blessing," he replied, shaking Chris's hand. "Gettin' ready for the snow, I see."

Both men glanced briefly at the overcast sky.

"We're supposed to see a foot or so over the next couple of days. Rachel and I can button up for a day or two if we have to. She has a pot of soup on. Have you had lunch?" asked Chris.

"I had a burger a little while ago, so I better pass, much as I like your wife's cooking," said Lyle. "Sheriff's deputy got those guys that you called about the other day. I did part of the investigation. They didn't have any licenses or carcass tags and the driver of the van had priors for dealing in exotic animals. I'm just guessing, but I bet that when we get the warrant and search his place in Farmington, we'll find a whole lot more. Anyway, those men poached those animals or bought 'em from someone who did and were planning on mounting them for sale. They might even have been items on a shopping list."

"Who on earth would buy this sort of stuff anyway?" asked Chris, shaking his head with a grimace. "I can't imagine hanging a head on my wall that I didn't kill. Hmmm…wonder if the buyers could be in trouble with the law too?"

"Those people are slippery, Chris. It isn't against the law to sell legally acquired trophy heads, so the buyer would admit only to answering a Craigslist or some other internet ad. Great White Hunter wannabes may be jerks, but being a jerk isn't illegal either," said Lyle, slowly wagging his head with a mournful smile. "And those guys spend some bucks. A seven-by-seven elk head might sell for $10,000, and I heard of a four-head grand-slam bighorn sheep collection going for $50,000. There were two mountain lion carcasses in the van too." Lyle continued, "Those go for $5,000 to $10,000, depending on the mount." Lyle turned toward his truck. "There's another wild card: the payoffs are big in the alternative medicine and food delicacy markets, too. The going rate for four black bear paws is around a thousand. Some of the Asians make soup out of 'em. Bear gallbladders are even more expensive. A deer carcass sells for a couple of hundred, just for the table. More money in poaching and black marketing than you might think.

"Anyway, I wanted to let you know about the bust. You might get a subpoena if this goes to trial. Depends on plea bargain offers and the aggressiveness of the defense lawyers. There might be a question of probable cause for stopping the van, but the County Mountie who made the stop is a buddy of mine." Lyle grinned broadly. "I'll bet he can find a taillight out or a license plate too muddy to read… something like that.

"Anyway, thanks for turning these bums in," Lyle continued. "Guys like that give us honest hunters a bad name. Ya know, I can understand a man shooting a deer to put meat on the table." His eyes twinkled. "Sometimes, a man down on his luck might take an illegal deer…he's gotta feed his family somehow. But dealing in trophies?" He shook his head. "I just can't see it."

"I never heard that," said Chris with a chuckle.

Lyle got in his truck, shut the door, and lowered the window. "I'll keep you up to speed with the court case. See ya."

He turned the truck around and drove back down the driveway.

*****

Chris's home was near the center of an area covered by a winter storm. He and his wife stayed home and kept themselves occupied with putting up fish, game, and canning the last apples of the season. Their pantries and freezers were full.

They had two high-clearance four-wheel-drive vehicles, so they could navigate the five miles to town through eighteen inches of snow if they had too, but other than checking the mail, there was nothing in town that they needed for a while. The power had stayed on and there was plenty of firewood and kerosene for backup if auxiliary heat and light were needed.

Chris stayed occupied with projects in his workshop—wood, leather, and metalwork; his wife sewed and worked on photograph manipulation on her computer. Satellite TV was usually reliable, and their music and DVD library along with plenty of books in print made for peaceful evening pastime. They cooked, talked, made love, enjoying each other in their winter solitude.

The bad weather finally passed on, and the roads became clear enough to permit safe automobile travel. Chris and his wife went to the grocery store in town for some fresh vegetables and to the post office to pick up their accumulated mail. They stopped at a coffee shop on the way home and sipped some hot chocolate while they opened their mail and read the local newspaper.

He read an article about a local court proceeding in which a group of men were being indicted for poaching, trafficking in illegally obtained wild game trophies, and conspiracies to do those things. These were likely to be the men that Chris had reported to the Sheriff's Department. The article described the magnitude of the monetary fines, which were substantial, and also mentioned the possibility of racketeering and computer fraud charges, which could result in imprisonment. Some illegally obtained hunting licenses had been found at one of the alleged poacher's homes, apparently fraudulently acquired online. Chris had known that the monetary penalties could be substantial but never considered the possibility of jail time; upon reflection, he realized that there was a quantum difference between taking an occasional illegal deer for food on the one hand and, on the other, repetitively slaughtering animals in money-making commercial enterprises, many in which the trophy taking was an end in itself; the carcasses were wasted, left to consumption by carrion eaters.

Chris had one set of antlers hanging on a wall in his den—antlers only. He had to ask himself if even this benign memento of a successful hunt which was carried out to provide food was morally acceptable. Perhaps it was similar to displaying a medal won in in athletic contest? And one might assert that antlers are esthetically pleasing. Arguable either way.

The article went on to say that the men were released on bail and that the trials for them would be scheduled for some time in the spring at the local county seat. He would be most interested in the outcomes.

*****

Chris and Lyle walked out of the courthouse, under the new-growth-laden cottonwood trees that bordered the sidewalk to the parking lot. Lyle had been called to testify, so he was on duty and therefore in uniform. He had driven his duty pickup truck and leaned against the driver side door as he chatted with Chris. The April air was chilly in spite of the clear sky, and both men pulled up their collars against the gentle breeze.

"Well, Chris, did they get their comeuppance?" asked Lyle.

"Yeah, I guess. Thousands of dollars in fines and some jail time is about fair. Lifetime loss of hunting privileges hurts too, but I doubt if these guys were ever sportsmen-type hunters anyway. They won't be able to make the big bucks the way they used to, though. And that all by itself is a win for the hunting community," said Chris.

Lyle smiled his mournful smile. "Racketeering is a Fed charge, so they'll spend some time in a minimum security facility. But I bet they'll be back in business in a year or two. You can take a goof off the street, but you can't take the street out of the goof."

"Well, maybe they'll see the light...we can always hope. Meantime, you have your hands full with enforcement. Don't envy you that job, ole buddy," said Chris, a serious expression on his face. "I worry about you, sometimes."

A woman and a man approached the two men, she holding a microphone and the man carrying a television camera. Lyle saw them coming, put his hands in his jacket pockets, and continued to lean back against his truck. The woman appeared to be in her late twenties or early thirties and was dressed in a dark business suit, white shirt, and thin black tie. Five foot four or so, her posture was erect, almost military. She was pretty with short swept-back blond hair, frosted at the tips. Her facial expression was serious, nearing pugnacious, but she was quite feminine in spite of her efforts to appear severe. The man was dressed in khakis and a windbreaker. Forties or fifties, graying at the temples, five foot ten or so, relaxed.

"This is Tamara Minsky reporting from the county courthouse where several big-game hunters have been convicted of poaching and trafficking in wild animal trophies and carcasses," said the woman, speaking into the microphone. "I'm approaching one of the wildlife officers that confidential sources have told me was instrumental in bringing this case to trial." She approached Lyle and held out her microphone as the cameraman filmed the encounter.

"Officer Thibodeaux, what can you tell me about this case?"

Lyle's face became long and somber. He paused for a moment as he stared at the reporter, glancing once at the cameraman, and said, "First of all, I need to correct something that you said. The men that were convicted today of the various offenses connected to poaching and trafficking in wild animal trophies today were not hunters. These men are thieves and scofflaws and aren't like any hunter that I know. They have stolen some of the wild animals that Americans like to view, to hunt, and to eat...they've stolen those animals from you and me and any other nature lover. Please don't refer to them as hunters."

The woman bridled and said, "These men were convicted of killing some trophy animals and attempting to sell them for profit. What do you call it if not hunting?"

She thrust the microphone even closer to Lyle's face.

"I call it trafficking, I call it dealing in stolen goods. These men killed quite a few game animals, beyond legal limits, without valid licenses, and out of season, and there's evidence that they left some of the carcasses to rot. That's assassination, not hunting," said Lyle, staring steadily at the reporter. "Hunting is a traditional pastime with some time-honored rules. State laws have refined and codified those traditional standards of behavior, and the Feds, right or wrong, have weighed in with some regulations of their own. So please don't ever confuse a poacher and a hunter. You might as well mistake a cow pie for a cheese danish."

Ms. Minsky sniffed and gave a brief shake of her head.

"Second, the successful prosecution of these men was a collaborative effort including Wildlife officials, state and county law enforcement, and federal law enforcement. No single person or group can lay claim to the outcome of this court case." Lyle glanced quickly at Chris and went on. "You need to be aware of the importance of citizen reports, too. Law enforcement is spread too thin to identify many offenders, and tips from hunters are invaluable. I got a call from a man who can legitimately be called a hunter about these men. He witnessed some suspicious activity and notified law enforcement and the Fish and Wildlife people. We got lucky with the collar and the rest is history."

Lyle glanced at the cameraman again, then back to the reporter. His eyes glinted, but he was able to muster a smile, frosty though it was, and said, "Will there be anything else?"

The reporter glared at Lyle and said, "Don't you think that if it weren't for the Endangered Species Act and PETA and other such laws and organizations, hunters would slaughter all of the wild game to extinction?"

She leaned toward Lyle again, stabbing the air near his face with the microphone.

Lyle smiled a friendlier smile and said, "Yeah, that's the party line anti-hunter position. There are some facts that suggest that the position isn't exactly right. The latest rendition of the Endangered Species Act was signed into law in 1970. PETA came into being in 1980. Far earlier and thanks to the activities and efforts of hunters, the Lacey Act was passed…that was in 1900. A rather famous hunter was instrumental in getting the Migratory Bird Act passed in 1901. Those are federal laws, and they have been amended and refined over the years. Outdoorsmen and hunters have been putting forth substantial efforts to preserve, to manage wildlife for a lot of years… long before it was stylish."

The reporter tightened her lips and shook her head. "I can't imagine any hunter that I would believe in, that I would trust."

Lyle continued to smile and said, "Well, maybe you should Google Teddy Roosevelt when you run out of things to do. By the way, when and where will this interview be aired? I'd really like to see it."

The reporter turned off her microphone and dropped it in her purse. She nodded toward the cameraman who lowered his camera.

"I don't know that it will be aired at all." She looked down and to the left, glanced back at Lyle. "I'll send it to some editors that might be interested, maybe documentary, maybe news, maybe print media. Frankly, your answers weren't quite what I expected. We'll see what the editors come up with."

"Well, I'll be tuned in. And in case you need any reminders, you can give me a call." He pulled the micro-recorder out of his jacket pocket, held it up between beefy thumb and forefinger, gazing at it for a moment, then back to the reporter. "I can fill in any blanks, anything you may not remember."

"You can't…" she stammered.

"Have a nice day, Ms. Minsky."

He touched his forehead in a casual salute and turned toward Chris. They walked a few steps away where they turned to watch the departure of the reporter and cameraman.

Chris asked, "Do people like that show up every time there's a poaching case in court?

"No," Lyle replied. "This case is a lot bigger than most of them, and once the Feds get into the show, the more media attention seems to be generated."

"How does this work, Lyle? Does this interview and the film footage belong to those two? How does it get broadcast?" asked Chris.

"I dunno, Chris. She's probably freelancing. I guess reporters send this stuff to some editors at some stations that they work with, and they accept or reject it. We'll find out soon enough. Can't say I'm too worried about it, though."

Lyle held up the micro-recorder again and laughed.

"Good thinking, Lyle," said Chris, chuckling.

They had arrived at Chris's pickup truck. He got in, brought down the window, and waved at Lyle as he started the engine.

"See ya soon."

Lyle raised a hand as Chris drove away.

*****

Chris parked in front of the cafe/deli and went inside. It was one o'clock, and the lunch crowd had thinned out a bit. He approached the display case near the order-and-pay counter and inspected the offerings. The young man behind the counter looked expectantly at him.

Chris said, "I'll have half of that ham and cheese on rye and a glass of unsweetened ice tea."

The young man looked at Chris nervously and said, "Uh...can't cut the sandwich."

A voice behind Chris said, "That's okay, I'll take the other half and some water."

Chris turned to find Tamara Minsky staring at him.

"Terrific," said Chris as he nodded to the young fellow. 'You can cut that guy in two, can't you?" as he dropped a $20 bill on the countertop. "This should cover it." To Ms. Minsky, he said, "Want to join me?"

She picked up the glass of water that had appeared on the counter, smiled at Chris, and said, "I was counting on it."

Chris chucked softly, looked Ms. Minsky in the eye, and said, "I'm Chris Walker."

He picked up his order and led the way toward a table by the window. It was a tall window, complimenting the high ceilings of the turn-of-the-century building, facing southwest and partially shaded by an enormous blue spruce.

"This look okay to you?" he asked.

She glanced at Chris then out the window at the trees and the mountains beyond. She expelled a deep sigh and said, "Yeah…yeah, this is nice…this place is just gorgeous."

She put down her plate, glass, and utensils and sat down. She watched Chris as he took his seat, glanced at her food, and slowly smoothed her napkin across her knees.

"Your friend, Officer Thibodeaux is quite a fellow. Always seems to have an answer. Guess he's heard those kinds of questions before."

She took a sip of water and primly dabbed her lips.

"Lyle is a sharp guy…could have gone to law school. Debate team captain, Phi Beta Kappa key from Stanford, and all that. He just decided that he liked outdoors better than indoors. He was a cop in LA for a few years, then came back to the mountains. Never looked back. He can play on my team anytime…or maybe he'll let me play on his," said Chris with a reflective stare out of the window. He looked back at Ms. Minsky with a shy smile. "An old friend, old hunting buddy. He and I and our wives used to get together quite a bit, until he…"

His face clouded over as his voice trailed off.

"So now he's a swinging single, eh?" said Ms. Minsky with a bitter smile.

"No, a not-so-swinging widower," Chris said, a deep wrinkle in his brow. "Sheila died of breast cancer a year or so back. Awful young for that, but breast cancer is an equal-opportunity heartbreaker. Lyle took it better than most men would, but he has his faith and good family and friends' support, so I shouldn't be surprised. He's a tough guy."

She looked down at the floor. "I'm sorry. I never would have figured…he just seems too young to be a widow. Any kids?"

Chris gave a brief shake of his head.

She nibbled at her sandwich and sipped some more water. She took a deep breath and looked at Chris. "I guess I don't understand the hunting thing, the personality type that is willing to kill for his dinner. I suppose I assumed that only a knuckle-dragging Neanderthal engaged in that sort of activity. I'm not a vegetarian, but something about killing my own food instead of getting it off the grocery store shelf seems sort of barbaric, sort of primitive. Not much of a hunting tradition in my family as you may have guessed, and there certainly wasn't at Sullins. I have to admit that I don't even know anyone who owns a gun."

"Yeah." Chris nodded slowly. "Hunting is barbaric in the sense that any violent death seems that way. But think for a minute about predators: wolves, lions, coyotes, hawks, and so on…consider how they survive…they kill their prey, claw and fang, usually in more gruesome ways than you'd like to think about. The concept of humane killing is something entirely human. Animals don't have any rules of moral behavior. Granted that they don't usually kill for kicks, but when they take their prey, it isn't a pretty thing to watch, at least not from the twenty-first century human point of view.

"The purity of the moment when a high velocity projectile hits the right spot on a game animal and results in a near-immediate kill: that's what the hunter strives for. Yes, it's direct and basic. There's no grocery store shelf, no middleman. The animal has died so that I can live, so that I can feed my family. Think about how that chunk of steak arrives on your plate at Morton's. That piece of meat is part of a production line process, without fanfare or celebration of the animal's life and death, as mundane and as exciting as blowing your nose." Chris paused, looked out the window, and went on. "Sorry, I get a little passionate about this stuff, but golly, it's wild and beautiful out there, and the animal is part of it. The deer that I kill has an elegance and dignity that domesticated critters will never have. From the hunter's perspective, there's a thrilling feeling of being really alive, of being intimately connected with nature. I can't tell you how it feels to walk around in the woods with a weapon in my hands, a pack on my back, breathing fresh air, and anticipating the shot that might

47

put fresh meat on the table for dinner. It's among the things I thank God for…" He looked down and blushed a little. "Sort of hard to describe."

They ate in silence for a few minutes.

Ms. Minsky cleared her throat. "You're a likable guy, Chris, and I don't want to annoy you, but how do I broach the subject? Any discussion about hunting has to eventually proceed to gun control." She looked out the window for a moment, took another deep breath, and said, "I wonder if the world wouldn't be a better place if we didn't have any guns at all."

Chris looked down, and the muscles in his jaws became prominent. He looked up at Ms. Minsky, his expression intense.

"We've been talking about hunting so far. I could learn to kill game animals for food without firearms. Long before guns were ever thought of, humans have used sticks and stones and traps to kill prey…and to kill each other. Firearms were invented to make both objectives more efficient. Objections to firearms or to any other weapon are really objections to human nature. There will always be people who are willing, eager even, to use violence as a means to deal with other folks, and they will use violence whether they have firearms or not. They threaten or do harm to other people because they are insulted or angry or because they want to prey on them, and the law abiding among us have to be able to defend ourselves. Law enforcement helps, especially against the more organized criminals. But police can't be there for us every time there is a confrontation… we wouldn't want so many cops around that they could be. So we have to be prepared to protect ourselves, and firearms are one way, one that I'm not willing to give up."

Ms. Minsky squirmed a little in her chair. She took a sip of water.

"What you're describing is pretty uncivilized."

"Uh-huh." Chris finally smiled. "Some members of our civilization don't act very civilized. That's just a fact of life that no legislation can change. It's fairly easy to stay away from the bad guys in a small town up here in the mountains. Harder to do in the inner cities."

Ms. Minsky glanced at her cell phone lying on the table as it emitted a tinkling bell tone. She punched a button on the lower part of the screen and peered at the display.

"Much as I am enjoying talking to you, I have an appointment in a half hour. Thanks for lunch. Maybe we can do this again another time?"

Chris smiled at her again. "Sure. Or maybe we can snag Lyle and my wife and go shoot some pheasant. Shouldn't be too hard to get you a hunting license. Wouldn't want to do anything illegal."

She stood, slid her purse strap over her shoulder, turned toward Chris with a wry smile, and said, "Maybe," as she strode toward the door.

Take a Pass

Jerry drove. Arty rode shotgun. Craig and Tim, being under-classmen, rode in the back seat. They had all participated in the high school football game which had been over for about an hour. Jerry and Arty were quarterback and backup respectively, Craig was a fullback, and Tim was a wide receiver who had come off the bench following an injury to the first stringer and caught a touchdown pass against their bigger, stronger archrival. The score had brought their team within one point of a tie. With less than a minute to go, their coach had opted for the two-point conversion which, having failed, denied them the upset win. The opponents then ran out the clock, frustrating the home team.

It was a cool September night, and they were on their way to a postgame party at a friend's house. They were riding in Jerry's Jeep Wrangler, highly modified and tricked out for off-road activity. Jerry was surly with his team's loss.

"We need to score some beer for the bash," he said, turning to Arty. "Do you have that fake ID that we used a couple of weeks ago?"

Craig and Tim looked at each other. Craig's stare cut away, and Tim squirmed in his seat, wiping his palms on his pant legs.

Arty shook his head. "Mom found it in my shirt pocket when she was washing clothes. Been grounded ever since 'til tonight."

They passed a pickup truck on the side of the road. Its occupant was talking on a cell phone. A couple of hundred yards past the pickup was a hitchhiker. He was middle-aged and unshaven. He carried a worn backpack.

"Got an idea," said Jerry, pulling the car to the side of the road beside the hitchhiker. He spoke through the open passenger window. "Where you headed?"

The hitchhiker bent at the waist, making eye contact with Jerry. "Just trying to get to the bus station at Crossroads Village."

Jerry nodded and said, "Tell you what: if you'll buy us some beer at the 7-Eleven in Crossroads Village, we'll get you to the bus station. We want a couple of six packs of malt liquor, and we've got the green."

He held up a $50 bill. The hitchhiker glanced down the road in the moonlight and pulled his coat a little tighter against the chill.

"Okay, guys. Just don't rat me out."

Arty got out of the jeep and opened the rear door.

"Scoot over, Tim, I'm comin' in."

The hitchhiker got in the front seat, closed the door, and Jerry drove away.

*****

The occupant of the pickup truck ended his phone call and watched the hitchhiker get into the metallic black shackled-up Jeep. Deputy Jimmy O'Neil thought for a minute. He was off duty and wasn't too keen on rousting a hitchhiker. He had enjoyed the football game earlier and wanted to get home where his wife had dinner waiting. He had, however, recognized the car—it belonged to the home team quarterback in the game he had witnessed earlier. He started the truck and turned onto the highway. He followed them seven miles into Crossroads Village and slowed as the Jeep parked in front of the convenience store. When the hitchhiker got out of the passenger seat and walked quickly into the 7-Eleven, Deputy O'Neil made his decision. He drove on about a quarter mile, then executed a U-turn and drove back to the convenience store. He parked near the Jeep a few spaces away and waited, raising his cell phone to his ear without making a call, and watching the convenience store entryway out of the corner of his eye.

The hitchhiker was carrying a large paper bag when he came out. He approached the Jeep, looked around nervously, and got into the front seat. They backed out of the parking space and proceeded onto the highway and into Crossroads Village toward the truck stop that served as a bus station. Deputy O'Neil followed a few car lengths back and turned into the parking lot of the truck stop soon after the sedan. The boys parked near the office area, and O'Neil stopped in a row of parking places directly behind the Jeep and shut off his head-lights. The hitchhiker got out of the front seat, carrying his backpack. The rear door opened, and Arty got out, said something to the hitch-hiker, laughing out loud, and got into the front seat. The hitchhiker hurried to the truck stop door. O'Neil started his truck, turned on his lights, and pulled forward to the back of the Jeep, nearly touching its rear bumper. He speed-dialed his cell phone.

"Dispatch, this is Deputy O'Neil requesting backup at Crossroads Village Truck Stop, four boys and one adult engaging in suspicious behavior."

Jerry saw the truck in the rearview mirror but couldn't see its occupant in the glare from the lights of the truck stop.

"Oh, shit! Somebody's got us blocked in."

A silky feminine voice said, "You're off duty, Deputy O'Neil. Scoring some overtime?"

O'Neil chuckled. "Just send a unit this way, Kathy."

"10-4, Deputy. WilCo."

O'Neil took his off-duty pistol from the ankle holster and put it in his right jacket pocket. He got his badge wallet from his hip pocket and put it in the other jacket pocket. He got out of the truck with his right hand in the jacket pocket and approached the blue sedan. Standing a little behind the door handle, he knocked on the window with his left hand. Jerry had been watching him since he got out of the truck. With trembling hand and a dry mouth, he brought the window down.

"Whatcha' need, fella?"

O'Neil took the badge wallet from his pocket, flipped it open for Jerry to see, and said, "Deputy O'Neil. I saw that you picked up a hitchhiker."

"Uh, yessir, we did," said Jerry. "Its cold out there and getting late, so we brought him down here to the bus station."

"Yeah. Right. I noticed that you made a stop at the 7-Eleven too." O'Neil ducked his head and looked past Jerry toward the floorboard on the passenger side of the sedan. "Wonder what's in that bag on the floorboard? Couldn't be something that the hitchhiker bought for you, could it?"

Jerry stammered. "I...I guess he accidentally left it here when he got out of the car." He turned toward Arty. "Arty, why don't you go inside and take that guy his stuff?"

Arty reached for the door handle just as a sheriff's vehicle, a sedan with lights flashing, cruised to a stop beside O'Neil's. A short young woman in uniform got out of the car. She strolled toward the passenger side of the Jeep and rapped gently on the window with her Maglite. Arty brought the window down and looked up at the deputy.

"Uh, hi there..." he said.

Deputy Karen Johnson made eye contact with Arty, then raised her eyes, smiling sweetly at O'Neil over the top of the car.

"What's the haps, Jimmy?"

O'Neil's eyes flicked toward Deputy Johnson and back toward Jerry.

"These boys picked up a hitchhiker on the road back toward Vista Grande. They stopped up the road at a 7-Eleven, and the hitchhiker went inside...came out with a big paper bag. Jerry here tells me that they brought the guy to the bus stop...funny thing is that when he went inside, he didn't have the big paper bag with him, just his backpack. Wonder if the boys got some payback for the ride...maybe something kids can't buy?"

Johnson switched her flashlight to her left hand, resting her right hand on the Glock 19 strapped to her right hip, and said, taking a step backward, "What's your name, young fella?"

"Uh…I'm Arty Berger, ma'am."

He glanced down, then back at the deputy. He didn't know what else to say.

"Why don't you exit the vehicle, Arty, and we can talk a little, okay?" she said, taking a further step back and to the rear of the sedan. "Nice and slow."

"By the way, good to see you, KK," said O'Neil. He looked back at Jerry, performed the same distancing maneuver as had Johnson, and told him to get out of the vehicle. "You boys in the back seat, stay where you are for now." To Jerry, he said, "I'll need to see your driver's license, easy does it. Turn around and put both hands on top of the car."

Jerry did as he was told.

O'Neil said, "Feet back farther, so you have to lean against the car."

Jerry complied.

O'Neil said, "Take out your wallet and drop it on the ground behind you."

O'Neil picked up the wallet and flipped it open. The driver's license was in a clear plastic compartment that was easily visible in the bright lights of the truck stop.

"Gerald Ambrose, age eighteen…starting quarterback, I believe. You oughta know better." He put the wallet in his pocket and flashed his Maglite on the occupants of the back seat. "Got some other team members in here too." He flashed the beam in Tim's face, then away, and said, "Nice catch in the end zone, especially for a rookie…bet you won't be warming the bench for long."

He turned off the light and said to Jerry, "What's in the paper bag, Mr. Ambrose?"

Jerry's voice quivered slightly. "I…uh…don't know. You'll have to ask the hitchhiker."

"Can you take a look in that bag, KK?" said O'Neil.

Arty was out of the Jeep by now and Deputy Johnson turned him around and cuffed his hands behind him. She then accompanied him to her squad car and put him in the back seat, closing the door.

She returned to the side of the Jeep and, keeping an eye on the boys in the back seat, picked up the paper bag from the floorboard and put it on the seat. She peered inside the grocery bag and saw two six-packs of malt liquor.

"Looks like somebody is planning a party tonight, Jimmy. Going inside to look for a hitchhiker."

"Roger that…be careful."

O'Neil cuffed Jerry and extracted the ignition key from the Jeep. Deputy Johnson went into the truck stop and spoke to the man behind the desk. She couldn't see anyone else.

"Did a guy come in here a little while ago and buy a bus ticket?" she asked, voice level.

The tall balding man behind the counter had both hands flat on the Formica. His eyes shifted left and right, and he cleared his throat. "There was a guy…bought a ticket for Denver…he was sitting right over there a while ago. Don't see him now."

"Back door?" asked Deputy Johnson.

"I keep it locked at night, but that don't keep people in, it just keeps 'em out."

"How about going into the men's john and see if anybody is in there?" she said.

"None of this is any of my business. If you want to know who's in there, you'll have to do it yourself," said the man, standing a little straighter.

The deputy stared balefully at the proprietor for a moment, grimaced, then walked down a corridor to the men's room, pushed open the door a little, and said, "Sheriff's Deputy Johnson here. Come on out of there so I can talk to you."

She waited thirty seconds or so, then said, "I'm coming in."

She walked into the restroom and moved the beam of her flashlight about, checking every corner and every stall. The room was empty. She exited the restroom and walked down the hall to the back door. It was unlocked and ajar. She pushed the door open a little with her left hand, right hand on the butt of her Glock, and peered through the narrow opening. Across the back parking lot, she could see the kiosk that served as the bus station. She could also see a passenger bus pulling out of the parking lot and onto the highway.

She considered running back to her car and chasing down the bus. It was likely that the hitchhiker was on board, but she would have to call in more backup to manage the collar. Vagrancy and contributing to the delinquency of minors, just for starters. And what would putting him in the county lockup for a month or two accomplish? She shook her head as she thought about the same old revolving door that the criminal justice system had become.

She locked the door and returned to the front of the establishment. The proprietor was still behind the counter, staring anxiously at her. She said, "You should be more careful about keeping that door locked. A fleeing felon just might be trying to get on a bus."

The man's eyes went wide, and he started to say something, thought better of it, and pursed his lips.

Deputy Johnson smiled at him and said, "Keep cool, neighbor."

She walked out the door. She strode across the parking lot and approached O'Neil.

"Looks like our perp boogied out the back door and made the bus. Doubt it's worth it trying to catch him on the other end. Besides, if we're gonna do any good tonight, it'll be for these boys."

O'Neil glanced at the taillights of the departing bus, subtly shook his head, and sighed deeply. He looked at Deputy Johnson with a smile.

"Yeah, let's get these guys down to the station and start calling parents."

*****

Chris Walker was working with a wood planer outside the doorway of his workshop on the cement apron. The overhead garage-style door permitted easy access to his workshop when he brought in lumber or sheets of plywood for whatever he was building. He used this space to process game animals too, so the generous doorway was useful in many ways. He was expecting a visitor soon. He had been approached by a friend asking him to spend some time with his son who had recently had a minor run-in with law enforcement. Chris's friend, Charlie Noland, was an over-the-road truck driver and spent a good bit of time away from home. His sixteen-year-old son needed more time with his dad, but until Charlie could carry out application and interviews for local-run trucking so that he could be at home every night, he thought that mentoring by his old hunting buddy, Chris, might be good for his son. Chris had agreed to help his friend, but pointed out that since he was not a parent, his ability to relate to a teenager might not be all that Charlie wanted. Charlie had laughed, slapped Chris on the shoulder, and said, "Don't worry, Chris, you'll both get something out of it."

The twelve-inch planer was an older model machine that was secured to a portable workbench with large metal clamps. Chris was wearing wraparound safety glasses and a set of earmuff-style hearing protectors. A stack of rough-cut four-quarters black walnut boards was leaning against the side of the garage, each between four and eight feet long. Chris fed them one at a time into the planer and walked around the unit to its out-feed area to receive each board as it finished its pass through the machine. A pile of planer shavings about a foot deep lay on the ground near the out-feed. It was tedious, brain-numbing work, shaving the lumber down, one-thirty-second of an inch at a time. It was a beautiful fall day to be outside, though, and the smell of the shavings was clean and a little sweet smelling. Chris smiled as he picked up the next piece of lumber. There were a dozen or so boards to be planed. They were eight inches to a foot wide and were destined to become a dresser, the photos for which were found in a magazine by Chris's wife. Chris had to draw up his own plans and materials list and chose some black walnut that he had been saving for just such a project.

The taxicab-yellow Jeep Wrangler turned into Chris's driveway and drove the one-eighth mile to his garage apron. A tall, stocky man with thick close-cropped gray hair stepped lightly out of the driver's door and waved at Chris. The passenger door opened, and an equally tall, lean teenager got out of the Jeep. They walked toward Chris, the older man smiling, the younger man looking at the ground. Chris shut off the planer and removed his hearing protectors, hanging them on the workbench. Charlie Noland walked up to Chris with outstretched right hand.

"Morning, Chris. How's it goin'?"

Chris took the offered hand. "Beautiful day in the mountains, Charlie. Fall's about here. Be hunting season soon." He turned to the teenager, extending his right hand. "This must be Tim. I'm Chris Walker."

Tim smiled shyly and took the Chris's hand. His hand was dry, and his grip was firm. He looked Chris in the eyes as he shook hands, then looked down at the ground again. Chris smiled at the young man, the skin by his eyes crinkling; this would work out okay.

"Like to help me do a little woodwork, Tim?" asked Chris.

"Uh, yessir, if you'll have me…" said Tim, glancing at the planer, then at Chris, then back to the ground again.

Chris turned toward Charlie. "Give us a couple of hours to get acquainted and do a little preliminary work. I'll bring the young fella home when we're through—got to get the mail in town and pick up some groceries."

Charlie gently punched his son on the shoulder and said, "Listen to this guy, and you might learn something."

He nodded toward Chris and turned back toward his jeep.

Chris motioned for Tim to follow him into the workshop. He pulled two stools together in front of a workbench where some furniture plans were scattered. He pointed to one of the stools and sat on the other one.

"These are some drawings that I made of the dresser that we're making. It's a fairly small one with three drawers, and it's only four feet high. My wife, Rachel, wants this one for the guest room, and the walnut matches the rest of the furniture."

Tim gazed at the plans. "How does it hold together…I mean, do you just put nails in it or what?"

Chris chuckled. "There are several different kinds of glue joints that'll go into this dresser, and I'll show you how to make them all. I don't use a lot of metal fasteners like nails or screws." He plucked another set of ear protectors and safely glasses off the tool array bolted to the wall, handed them to Tim, and said, "But before we start putting things together, we have to plane the boards and trim and square the edges. Let's get back outside to the planer."

Chris was pointing out the features of the planer and explaining to Tim how the machine worked.

"There is a cylinder in the upper portion of the planer that has two blades in it called a cutter head. It revolves at a high rate of speed, and the whole upper portion of the tool is raised or lowered by rotating this handle. To bring the cutting head down onto the board, you would turn the handle counterclockwise."

Chris rotated the handle a little by way of demonstration.

Tim looked confused and asked, "What's counterclockwise?"

Chris laughed and said, "I bet your folks have an analog clock in the house, you know, the kind with a long hand and a short hand."

Tim said, "Yessir, there's one like that in the living room. The clocks in my room have numbers on 'em…no hands."

"Right," Chris said, "Lots of clocks nowadays are digital, like the ones in your room or the one on your wrist. The old-timey clocks and watches have the two hands that rotate from the top where the twelve is to the right, and that direction is called clockwise. Think of driving a screw into a board with a screwdriver. The direction is the same as clockwise, and if you're spinning a nut onto a bolt, the phrase to remember is 'righty, tighty; lefty, loosey.'"

Tim laughed. "So to lower the cutting head its 'lefty, loosey'?"

"Right," said Chris, "and for a wide board like most of these"—he pointed to the boards leaning against the wall—"especially if they're hard wood like walnut, the cutter head needs to be brought down in small increments, small bits, or the machine will bog down and come to a stop. Planing hard wood takes a while, depending on how rough-cut the pieces are, because you can plane off no more than just a little bit at a time."

Chris put on his safety glasses and ear protectors, as did Tim, and switched on the machine. He pointed to the out-feed end of the planer where Tim stationed himself and fed the first board into the infeed ramp. Tim grasped the board as it protruded from the out-feed, and Chris made a palm-down damping motion with his hand. Tim nodded and pulled on the board more gently. As the board finished its pass through the machine, Chris turned it off and pulled his ear protectors down around his neck.

"Good going, Tim. You knew not to force the board through the planer by pulling too hard on it. Good instincts."

Tim blushed slightly and looked at the driveway.

"We'll do all of these boards two or three times 'til they're smooth and then the same on the other sides, okay? We want 'em all to be the same thickness. Just stack the boards on the ground with the side that we just planed up, then we'll move 'em all at once."

Tim nodded. They finished the planing in about a half hour.

They carried the boards to the inside of the workshop, then returned to the planer. Chris handed Tim a dustpan with a long vertical handle while he wielded a broom. The shavings from the planer were dumped into a nearby trash can, and the planer was partially disassembled and taken into the shop where it was stored in an under-counter cabinet. They returned to the workbench and planned some rough measurements of the components of the dresser. They measured the lengths of the sides and tops and selected the boards for width, grain pattern, and color. Chris pointed out the features of the table saw and of the jointer, and he and Tim cut the boards to rough size, then squared and smoothed the edges on the jointer. They somehow naturally fell into a system, whereby Chris would carry out a cut or a jointer pass, then hand the next board to Tim who would carry out the same procedure. They would shut off the machines and talk about each cut, refining Tim's technique as needed.

Chris looked at his watch. "Its four o'clock, Tim. Better sweep up and get you home."

Tim glanced at the clock on the wall. "Wow, time goes by in a hurry out here…didn't know it was getting so late."

Chris laughed and handed Tim the dustpan.

"Yep, time passes faster when you're concentrating."

*****

61

Charlie Noland and Chris spotted each other walking in opposite directions in the post office corridor that provided access to the mailboxes. The gloomy November weather outside darkened the interior of the building, distorting the hour of the day. They shook hands. Chris noticed the serious expression on his friend's face.

"You okay, Charlie? You look a little down in the mouth."

Charlie shook his head briefly. "Tim has a ball game this Friday, and I'm worried about the postgame activities. Since he went to first string back in September, he's gotten a little cocky. No misbehavior yet, but I see some clouds gathering."

"Gosh, Charlie, I haven't seen anything like that when Tim comes out to the workshop. He listens, he asks smart questions, and as far as performance is concerned…well, like his athletic activities, he's a natural. I see your son as one of those sharp youngsters that somehow seems to do everything well and some things in superior, even creative, ways." Chris looked down and shuffled a foot. "I wonder how you can reward a kid like yours in ways that encourage the type of behavior you want to see?"

"Don't know, Chris…I mean, I know that I want my boy to be a gentleman and a straight-thinking, sober adult, but I can't force him to do any of that, and I'm afraid that if I lean too hard on him, restrict his activities too much, it'll just make him rebellious. I remember what it was like when my dad leaned on me, and I didn't like it. Don't want to make the boy hate me."

Charlie looked down and shook his head.

"Yeah…well, I'd say you turned out okay. It's a breeze from my end, Charlie." Chris grabbed his friend's elbow, squeezing it briefly. "I can be Tim's buddy…you have to be his dad…not easy, and it'll be awhile before you can be his friend. Hey." Chris snapped his fingers and stared hard at Charlie. "I wonder if you could suggest throwing a postgame party at your house and invite the whole team. Everyone will know up front that what you are offering is a drug- and alcohol-free celebration of the football season. You could pick parents of a couple of Tim's teammates, folks you know that aren't likely to be permissive, as additional chaperones. I imagine that the idea of a party with chaperones is antique and not real popular one with the youngsters these days, but it worked when I was a kid. Anyway… something to think about."

Charlie raised his eyebrows, listening intently to Chris.

"Gosh, Chris, I don't know how I'd go about it…maybe talk to my wife, see what she thinks."

Chris chuckled. "Yeah, you'll want to do that first. Might want to talk to the coach too."

"Worth a try anyway," Charlie replied, pursing his lips. "Thanks, Chris."

They shook hands and went to their respective mailboxes.

*****

Tim picked up another piece of pizza and took a bite. He offered a piece to the pretty blond girl standing beside him and took a long drink of root beer.

"Wow," he said, "terrific pizza. Glad we got a piece before Craig ate it all." \The crowd of young people around the picnic table all laughed as Craig held up a crust that he had been gnawing on.

"Hey, Noland, takes some energy to block for our super-fine wide receiver—got to keep the tank full," he said, as he stuffed the remainder of the crust in his mouth.

The group laughed again.

"Awesome catch on that last pass, Noland. 'Bout time we beat Parkland."

They all milled around the table and the blazing firepit nearby, laughing and eating. Music came from a boom box across the patio. A few couples danced.

Tim took another sip of his root beer. "Yeah, Ambrose was on time with his passes tonight…feels good, doesn't it?"

"Uh-huh," said Craig, "but your last couple of catches really made him look good. Hadn't been for that high jump on that last play, we'd have lost to Parkland…again."

"Yeah, well, Jerry was trying to put the ball where no one but me could catch it." Tim looked down, then glanced at the young lady standing beside him who was gazing at him with undisguised adoration. He shuffled a foot and said, "Maybe the pass was a little high, but what the hey? I caught it. Be nice to get to the playoffs."

The crowd of kids murmured their approval.

The team's head coach was chatting amiably with Charlie Noland, looking around at all of the teenagers that had showed up at the postgame party. There were about forty of them.

"Turned out to be a great idea, Charlie…I'd have never believed that this sort of get-together would be so well attended," said Coach Abbott.

Charlie shook his head. "I can't believe it either. A buddy put a bug in my ear, so I thought I'd try it. I have to tell you, though, your approval, your being here made all the difference in the world. Doubt if they'd have showed up if you hadn't been all in."

Coach Abbot nodded. "They're a good bunch of kids, but as every Mom and Dad knows, it's a good idea to keep an eye on 'em. Some of the boys that are likely to misbehave haven't showed up tonight…I pretty much know who the bad boys are. We'll see."

A small group of teens approached the outside of the gate in the fence surrounding the patio where the party was going on. Jerry Ambrose, Arty Berger, another young man, and their dates opened the gate and stepped into the patio area. Charlie Noland took a step in their direction when Coach Abbott touched his shoulder.

"Let's see how Tim handles this."

Charlie paused, glanced at the coach, then at his son, then turned back toward the coach, nodding.

Tim spotted the newcomers and moved toward the entry area.

"How's it goin', Jerry?" He nodded at Arty and the other young man. "Glad you got the team invite." He stepped closer to Jerry. The odor of alcohol on his breath was unmistakable. "No booze at this party, though."

Tim gazed at Jerry directly, a smile on his face.

Jerry's expression turned briefly cold, then he glanced at Coach Abbott who was watching the exchange, smiled broadly at Tim, and said quietly, "Just had a sip or two at another party. Thought we'd come by and make an appearance. Most of the team is here anyway…"

His voice trailed off.

Arty took a step forward. "A piece of that pizza sure would go down easy, Tim. Can of Pepsi sounds good too. How 'bout it, Tim? Got space for your teammates?"

Tim glanced back at his dad and his coach, then at Jerry and Arty. "Beer breaks training. You want to risk talking to the coach tonight? We're gonna need you guys in the playoffs."

Arty raised his eyebrows, grabbed Jerry by the shoulder, pulling him toward the gate.

"Yeah, Tim," he said in a voice a little louder than it needed to be. "Our folks want us home early tonight…just wanted to stop by and say hello…see ya Monday." He herded his group toward the gate and waved at Coach Abbott. "Good game, Coach. See ya next week."

The coach raised a hand, a thin smile on his face, as the group departed, closing the gate behind them.

Tim glanced at his dad as he made his way back to the picnic table. He punctuated the moment with a smile and a wink.

Coach Abbott and Charlie looked at one another and simultaneously laughed.

"Yep," said the coach, "your get-together for the team was a good idea."

"Right," said Charlie. "We ought to make a habit of it."

Climbing High

The trail wound along atop a sharp ridge that connected an alpine meadow below to the base of the main peak of the mountain. It was well traveled but covered with loose rocks of various sizes and a little icy in places. The drop-off on either side was steep, extending a few hundred feet below to the shoulder of the ridge on each side, gradually becoming less steep as it blended into the trees. He had room on the narrow path to plant his hiking sticks with each step, but the tips did not penetrate well, sometimes skittering over larger pieces of broken granite. His pack, though light and compact, was felt as an unfamiliar heaviness across his shoulders, and when a pole tip skidded, he was slightly off balance. When hiking ridges like this one, his continuing fear was always that he would slip on the scree and fall down the steep bank; an old friend had died that way a few years ago. He was thinking of Richard when a pole slipped, and he was a little too off balance to recover...he felt himself falling...

*****

Chris woke in a sweat, confused with sleep, disoriented momentarily, his thoughts clearing gradually as he sat upright in bed. He glanced over at his wife, still sleeping soundly, then turned to his bed stand and located his clock by feel, turning off the alarm. It was set for 5:00 a.m., ten minutes from his startled awakening.

He quietly slipped out of bed and went downstairs, closing the doors to the second floor. He wiped his brow as he opened the door of the woodstove, feeling the cold morning air on his face and his scalp. He thought about his recurrent dream once again. He had never had such a dream before Richard's death. It occurred regularly, just before he was preparing for a climb. Mildly disconcerting. Good reason to keep on hiking.

A few coals remained in the stove. Some pieces of kindling and a couple of logs piled on the residual from last night's fire flamed up nicely.

After breakfast and coffee, Chris dressed for hiking with multiple layers suitable for the mid- September high country. His plan for the hike was to climb one of the high peaks and be home by midafternoon, so the pack required for this outing did not have to accommodate overnight equipment. He needed a change of clothes, water, lunch, and emergency/first aid kit. Lighter is better. He retrieved the sandwich that he had prepared the night before from the refrigerator and put it along with an apple and several energy bars in one of the exterior pockets on his daypack. Rain gear, rope, flashlights, spare socks, wool gloves and leather gloves, and maps were already in the pack, and Chris inventoried them once again. Two quarts of water were tucked into pockets designed for that purpose on either side of the pack. He checked his cell phone for battery status and, finding it adequate, put the phone in one of the protected interior pockets of the pack. The hike that he had planned was along a well-established series of trails, but Chris packed away his GPS unit anyway, just in case. He jotted a short note to his wife, reminding her of his planned itinerary, and put it beside her coffee cup and the covered plate of eggs and bacon that he had prepared along with his own breakfast. He put his pack in the car and opened the garage door.

The drive to the trailhead through the twilight starlit morning took about an hour, putting him there a little before 7:00 a.m. The sun had not yet risen over the eastern mountain range, but there was a little light. There were still occasional thunderstorms in the afternoons this time of year, in spite of the cooler temperatures, and experienced hikers were always attuned to weather changes. Getting off the mountain on the descent, at least below the tree line, by early afternoon was a longstanding habit. Being anywhere near a lightning strike on an exposed mountainside was a dangerous situation to be avoided.

As Chris drove west across the valley, he crossed the river through riparian cottonwood and willow woods, on through piñon pine high desert, then ponderosa and Douglas fir forest. The trailhead was located in the subalpine lodgepole pine/aspen zone at about ten thousand feet.

He parked his car in the generous-sized parking area. There was another vehicle in the lot. It had frost on its windshield.

Chris pulled off his running shoes and pulled on his hiking boots over his thick wool socks. He laced them snug but not tight, reminding himself that he would have to tighten things up on the descent. The temperature was twenty-seven degrees Fahrenheit, so he pulled on a woolen watch cap and stuffed his bill cap into his pack. He put on his wool gloves and his pack, tweaking the adjustment straps until it felt just right. The hiking poles in the back seat were already adjusted for Chris's height, arm length, and the uphill portion of the hike. Still, he grasped a pole in each hand, planted the points in the soft dirt of the parking lot, and did a deep knee bend. Satisfied with his equipment, he moved toward the trailhead.

The weathered wooden rail fence surrounding the parking area had an entryway gap near its center that marked the beginning of the trail. There was a sign there giving the name of the mountain and the mileage to the top—3.9 miles over about 4,000 feet vertical gain. Chris glanced at his watch, yanked at his shoulder straps one last time, and set off up the trail.

The trail began with a gradual ascent for about a quarter mile through the mixed pine and aspen, then becoming steeper, requiring switchbacks for the next quarter mile. The trail was dirt and pebble, but there was a blanket of pine needles and aspen leaves that softened any sound. The silence was nearly a living thing: the soft crunch of footfall seemed intrusive.

Chris stopped at the "bench" at the top of the switchbacks, a relatively flat area that extended a couple of hundred yards before the next climb. He changed hats, having warmed up a bit on the steeper terrain. He guzzled a half-pint of water and chewed up about half of a granola bar. After a few calf stretches on a downed log, he adjusted his pack's shoulder straps once again and set out along the bench.

Several more sets of switchbacks, benches, twists and turns, and a couple of creek crossings brought him to scattered areas of snow piled up on the north side of trees and the clumps of sagebrush. The trees were all spruce now and were thinning out as the tree line neared. The closer that Chris got to the bare mountain face beyond the tree line, the more stunted and deformed were the spruce. Flag trees. The wintertime high wind and extreme cold were harsh at this altitude and not conducive to the development of the symmetrical cone of a Christmas tree.

When Chris came to an area where the trees were sparse, he found a rock to sit on and pulled off his pack. He switched hats again, the temperature having dropped a bit with the increased altitude. The light breeze was more palpable now without the protection provided by the woods. The remaining piece of granola bar tasted wonderful, washed down with another half-pint of water.

He consulted a map in order to remind himself of the details of a trail that he had not traveled recently. A broad area of alpine meadow extended maybe a quarter mile ahead, then narrowed into a ridge that fell off on the north side, a steep drop extending a couple of hundred feet or so to an avalanche-generated field of scree and boulders at the base before the terrain leveled out. The sky was clear, but the wind had come up a bit more, a subtle keening sound waxing and waning with the breeze. Shouldering his pack once again, he set off uphill.

The minimal alpine vegetation was thinning out as he approached the rockslide area. The trail wasn't marked, but footfall of untold numbers of hikers and animals had pounded the small rocks and scree into a shallow rut that was easy to follow. The wind paused for a few minutes, and in the relative silence, Chris heard a faint whistling sound. Marmot maybe? He stopped and listened for a minute, and the whistling sound occurred again. No, not marmot. He walked along briskly, looking down the steep slope to the north. He covered fifty yards, scanning the slope periodically while keeping an eye on his footing. A flash of red appeared briefly, maybe fifty yards down the slope. It happened so fast that Chris wasn't sure that he had seen anything, but then the splash of color appeared fleetingly again. A sleeve. A coat sleeve. Someone waving an arm.

Chris pulled off his glove, put his fingers in his mouth and whistled, long and loud initially, then a few short blasts. He heard or saw nothing for a few minutes, and just as he was preparing to whistle again, he heard a weak cry for help. He cupped his hands around his mouth and yelled out, "Hold on, buddy, I'll get down as fast as I can."

He listened intently but heard no response. He got his mobile phone out of his pack and powered it on. One bar. He got out his GPS and powered it on too. The unit took a while to initialize, then finally displayed a map of his location. It obediently showed a pin at his location with lat/long readout near the bottom of the screen. His first attempt at dialing 911 failed, as did the second and third. He put his cell phone in an interior pocket close to his skin while he took off his pack and found the rope. The rope was three-eighth-inch nylon braid, 150 feet of it. His hiking buddies teased him about the extra four pounds that he probably didn't need to carry, and most of the time, they were right. Not this time.

He took out the mobile phone and tried 911 again. A voice answered on the third ring and demanded to know what was his emergency. The voice crackled and hissed. Chris began with "Climber down" and read the latitude/longitude from the GPS. Receiving no response, he repeated his call twice more. He waited for a response and was rewarded with a message on the phone display, "Call Failed." He tried several more times but was unable to make contact.

He sat down on a rock and thought. The time now was mid-morning. If Search and Rescue had gotten his message at all, their response time would be at least four, maybe five hours. He decided. Better get on down there.

He tied one end of the rope around the base of the rock that he was sitting on and coiled the rest in a loose configuration that he would sling over his shoulder. He tightened the straps on his pack, paying special attention to the straps that secured his water bottles. He put away his wool gloves and got leather gloves out of his pack. He tried calling 911 once again, then tried his home, neither successful. The scattered high cirrus clouds were combining into maybe fifty-fifty cloud cover. The wind was mild but chilly. Time to go. He shortened his poles and strapped them to his pack. He put on his pack, slipped the rope over his shoulder, and whispered a prayer.

He planted a foot against the rock around which the rope was secured and found that he was unable to move it. Good. Putting some tension on the rope, he backed over the precipice, looking over his shoulder ever so often, stopping to pay out some rope, and slowly working his way down the forty-five-degree slope. The surface was composed of scree and various sizes of rocks. He was able to navigate a fairly straight line toward the area where he saw the flash of red, but as he proceeded down, he became less certain of his ultimate destination. He slipped once on the crumbling scree and rolled onto his shoulder. A reminder to move slowly.

Chris stood tall, maintaining tension on the rope and surveyed the terrain below. He saw movement off to his right and further down the slope. Reestablishing grip on the rope, he crabbed sideways, moving slowly and deliberately in that direction. He shouted out, "Comin' to ya, buddy. Gimme a yell."

He heard a groan and a stifled sob coming from behind a boulder nearby. As he approached the boulder, he could see the red jacket sleeve, motionless now. Moving closer, he saw the young man lying on his back, feet downhill, his left arm held at a right angle to his torso. There was blood on his forehead, and the knees of his quilted nylon pants were shredded. He groaned and moved his head from side to side, panting. He was medium height and lean, maybe in his mid-twenties.

"Talk to me, pal…tell me where you're hurt," said Chris, his voice a little higher than usual, scrambling sideways across the rocky slope.

"Can you wiggle your feet…does your neck hurt…what's your name?"

He realized that he was talking too much. He clenched his jaw and moved closer. He knelt by the young man feeling for his pulse on a bare right wrist.

"What's your name, fella?" he asked as he loosened the straps on his pack.

The young man groaned again and croaked, "Bill, Bill Archer… my shoulder's killing me." He took a deep breath and met Chris's stare. "Sure got cold last night."

"Yeah, I bet it did. Does anything else hurt? Your neck or your back?"

He leaned across Bill's torso and felt the pulse at his left wrist. He rotated the forearm a little, and the young man groaned and said, "Don't move it! Don't move my shoulder!"

He groaned again and made a half-hearted attempt to reach his left shoulder with his right hand.

Dislocated, thought Chris.

"Ever hurt that shoulder before?" he asked. He inspected the shredded pant legs at the knee and found one to be bloody, the other not externally so.

"Yeah, I did it in a rock-climbing accident a few years back… damn, it hurts."

"Anything else, Bill? How about your neck?"

Chris reached down and pulled the toe of Bill's right boot gently upward, toward his head, and noted with satisfaction that he resisted the movement with pointing of his toe the other way. Chris performed the same maneuver with the other foot and with the same results. He nodded, saying, "Hmm," to himself. He took off his glove and slid his hand under Bill's neck.

"That hurt if I poke around your neck? No?" he said as Bill slowly shook his head. He pressed his palms to the side of Bill's chest.

"That hurt at all?"

Bill shook his head.

Chris moved around to Bill's left side. He tried calling 911 again and again saw the "No Service" message on his cell phone.

"Your shoulder's dislocated, Bill. Now we can wait for mountain rescue to get here, maybe with some pain drugs, but that might be hours from now, if they come at all. I can try to put it back in joint for you, but I don't have anything strong to give you for pain. If you're willing to try and we go slow enough, we might make it."

"Okay," said Bill through clenched teeth. "Same way they did it last time. I shoulda got it fixed…just didn't want to take the time."

"I'm going to ease your arm down, very slowly, so it's pushed into your side, then we're going to flex your elbow and rotate your forearm outward 'til it pops back in joint. We can do this if we go slow enough, especially since you've done it before. You ready to give it a try?"

Chris took hold of Bill's wrist and applied some gentle traction as he slowly moved the arm closer to his side. When Bill would groan especially loud, Chris would stop moving the arm while maintaining traction at his wrist, wait a few seconds, and continue slowly bringing the arm closer to Bill's side. When his elbow was in contact with his flank, Chris put his elbow in ninety degrees of flexion and slowly started to rotate the arm outward. Bill groaned periodically as the forearm neared parallel with the ground. The last inch or so of outward rotation was accompanied by Bill's cry of pain and a satisfying clunk that Chris felt more than heard as the shoulder fell back into its socket.

"Damn, what a relief, damn…" Bill sighed.

"Now don't try to move it, Bill. I'm going to tie your elbow around your torso so you can't fall and dislocate it again. Okay?"

Chris took the rope that he had used to descend the slope and, using his pocketknife, cut a four-foot length from its end. He pushed the end of the rope under Bill's back and tied a loose square knot, securing the loop to his torso. He took the two ends and tied them in a similar fashion around his arm snuggly, just above his elbow.

Chris retrieved one of his water bottles from his pack and put it in Bill's hand. He helped him come to a sitting position and guided the nozzle of the water bottle toward Bill's face. Bill needed no further encouragement. He wolfed down about half of the quart of water without stopping.

Chris pulled Bill's hood out of its pocket on his jacket and pulled it over his head.

"Wanna try getting up?" he asked. "Maybe if we take our time, we can crawl up this slope back to the ridge? Get you home for supper, maybe."

Bill smiled and nodded, looked around. "Not sure how I can get up with one arm."

He rolled to his right, coming to his knees, grimacing, supporting his torso with his right arm.

Chris looked up the mountain, then back at Bill. He took off Bill's tattered pack and tied it to the end of the rope that snaked up the slope.

"Here's what we'll do, Bill. I'll go first, get some tension on our lifeline. Once I get stood up, we'll stand you up next and get you a good grip on my pack. Then I do hand-over-hand up the slope… You're the caboose. Set your feet for every step, and if you feel yourself falling, try to roll toward your right side."

Chris looked at Bill and was relieved to see eye contact, a terse nod, and a determined expression. Chris stood, tightened the climbing rope, set his feet, and extended a right hand to Bill who took it and came shakily to his feet. He weaved a little then braced his feet, shifted his grip to one of the straps hanging from Chris's pack, and said, "Okay…good to go."

"If we can stay sort of in step, it'll probably work better."

Chris pulled his hat down, flexed his fingers, and took the first step.

For the first twenty feet or so, their progress was limited by poor coordination in the awkward and unfamiliar gait. Chris was pulling the two of them up the slope and had to pause ever so often to rest and check on Bill. The first stumble and fall occurred when a rock rolled under Chris's foot. The only good news was that the fall was to the right, and of course, Chris took Bill down with him, Bill rolling onto his good shoulder.

"You okay, Bill?" said Chris.

Bill chuckled. "I've had worse bites from the old slope snake. This would have been my forty-third fourteener, so I'm used to some bruises."

He waited to Chris to stand and steady himself, then pulled on Chris's pack strap in the process of getting to his feet. They paused for a few seconds, then resumed the slow progress up the slope.

In a half hour, after two more falls, they had reached the path along the ridge. Bill sat down on the rock that anchored the rope, and Chris handed him a water bottle. He retrieved the climbing rope slowly, the pack attached to its end snagging rocks and gullies in its progress up the slope.

He opened his pack and retrieved a medicine bottle containing some ibuprofen. He shook out two of the tablets and offered them to Bill.

"Not allergic to anything?" he asked and, seeing Bill shake his head, dropped the pills in his hand. "Not very strong stuff, but it might help some."

He gave Bill a granola bar and took the last one for himself. He stowed the coiled rope in his pack and tied Bill's pack to his own. Each of his hiking poles had to be adjusted for his and Bill's respective heights. He retrieved his cell phone once more and was again not able to establish contact. He tightened his boot laces. They were ready to start down the mountain.

The sky had become even cloudier, and the temperature had dropped a few more degrees. Chris helped Bill to his feet, snugged up the straps on his pack, and set off at a slow pace, leading the way along the ridge.

They reached the tree line in an hour or so and stopped to rest. They finished off the last of the water and stowed the bottles.

"How're you holding up, Bill? Having much pain?"

Bill shook his head. "Not bad as long as I don't try to move my arm. Getting pretty tired, though." He barked a short laugh. "Didn't get much sleep last night."

"I'll bet," said Chris. "Dinner and a warm place to sleep are gonna feel mighty good tonight."

They got their gear together and resumed the slow progress down. In an hour or so, they were nearing the switchbacks when they heard voices downhill. In a few minutes, some hikers came into view. There were four of them, all in orange jackets, the two in the back carrying a litter between them. The two men in front both had bulky backpacks. Chris hailed the rescue party and stopped to rest. He and Bill sat on a log near the trail and waited.

The man at the head of the foursome loosened his pack as he approached them.

"Did you guys call Search and Rescue? You both look pretty spry."

Bill and Chris introduced themselves.

"Yeah," Bill said, "I took a fall down the ridge trail late yesterday. This fella got me back up the slope a few hours ago." He glanced at Chris. "I was sure glad to see him. Hope we didn't put you guys to too much trouble."

The leader, Seth, introduced himself and took off his pack. "We got the call a few hours ago. The message was garbled. Made out enough of the lat/long part of the 911 call to make some educated guesses. Got lucky picking the right fourteener. Glad to see that you did okay without us."

He got out a blood pressure cuff and a small cubical instrument. He loosened Bill's jacket and the rope securing his left arm. He applied the blood pressure cuff and clamped the pulse oximeter to Bill's forefinger.

"How bad does that arm hurt you, Bill?" he asked, looking over Bill's scraped forehead and torn pant legs.

"Dislocated my shoulder again. This guy"—Bill gestured toward Chris—"put it back where it belongs. Then he got us up the slope to the ridge."

Seth looked at Chris. "Where'd you learn that? You a paramedic or a doc or what?"

Chris laughed. "Not by a long shot. A buddy I used to ski with kept dislocating his shoulder, so he had me stand by in the ER and watch the doc fix him. Next time he did it, I put it back on the spot. Saved him a trip to the hospital and a lot of pain. Never thought that the maneuver would come in handy ever again."

Seth nodded while he was repeating Bill's blood pressure. He did his paramedic-style survey and then stowed his instruments in his pack.

"Pressure's looking okay, a little low, but okay. Oxygen is good too. Let's get you off the mountain. You up for walking or do you want to ride the litter down?"

Bill stretched his shoulders, wincing. "I walked up, I'd rather walk down too. Got anything to eat in that pack…I'm starved."

Seth chuckled and opened his pack. He got out two envelopes of MREs.

"Spaghetti or pork sausage?"

Bill opted for spaghetti and quickly dispatched the contents of the MRE envelope along with a quart of water. Seth immobilized Bill's shoulder with a splint-type device that fit around his torso in the same way that Chris's jury-rigged rope had done.

"You'll be a little unsteady without the use of that left arm," said Seth, "so stay close to one of us and use your hiking pole…that third leg might save you a fall. Let's put me in the lead, you next, then Chris, then the rest of my crew. sound okay?"

Both men nodded. Chris put on his pack that still had Bill's gear tied to it and did a knee bend.

"Ready to go here. How about you, Bill?"

"Let's get outta here," said Bill, coming to his feet.

They started down the trail and into the switchbacks, Bill stopping every ten minutes or so. Another hour and a half brought them to the trailhead.

*****

Chris rapped on the door in the patient room area of the hospital. He pushed open the door that was ajar.

"Anybody home?"

"Come on in," said Bill. "Check out my new digs."

Chris took the offered right hand. "Pretty fancy. That bed looks like something out of a sci-fi movie."

Bill laughed. "Yeah, but I'd opt for home anytime. The doc says they'll cut me loose later today. The MRI of my shoulder showed some ligament damage, so I'll have to get it fixed some time or other. Maybe late in the spring, after ski season is over. When I said that to the doc, he rolled his eyes. Guess it's easier to dislocate a shoulder every time it happens." Bill shook his head and looked down at the splint as though it were an alien being. "This damn thing is about enough to convince me to do it sooner. Sure hate to give up a ski season."

"You might be able to get away with a brace for a while, just not forever. That buddy of mine I told you about finally got his fixed. Haven't seen him on the mountain without his brace."

Chris stood and lightly punched Bill on his good shoulder. "Glad to see you perked up. Keep in touch."

He reached for his shirt pocket and handed Bill a scrap of paper.

"Here's my email and phone number. Give me a call sometime, and we'll go get a beer and some pizza."

Bill's expression became serious as he looked up at Chris.

"Can't thank you enough, Chris. I owe you one."

Chris smiled. "Pay it forward, Bill. There's always somebody that needs a hand."

Ice and Memories

One of the remarkable things about high mountain lakes in the wintertime is the silence. There are no birds singing, there isn't much wind on a nice day, and the snow-covered terrain acts like insulation that dampens man-made noise. Usually quite peaceful. Occasionally, however, when fishermen are about, the silence is broken by the cacophonous racket of an ice auger. These oversized drills are powered by what is essentially a chain saw engine and are designed to punch holes in the ice pack for fishing.

Chris wrestled the auger into position on the ice, started the engine on the ungainly tool, and leaned hard on the handles as the machine clattered on, gradually penetrating a foot and a half of ice, leaving a pile of ice shavings around the hole. He withdrew the machine from the hole and drilled another one about three feet from the first. He shut the machine off and set it aside. The shavings beside each hole had to be cleared away, and the bits of ice floating on the water in the new holes had to be dipped out with a device that looked like a cooking strainer—an ice sieve.

He had hauled his auger, tent, fishing gear, and a cooler full of snacks and sodas onto the ice on an elongated sled-like tub designed for that purpose. He was alone on the ice this early January morning, for now. Other fishermen would be coming along soon. His pickup truck was parked about a quarter mile away on the shore of the lake. Later in the season, when the ice was perhaps more secure, some fishermen would drive their vehicles onto the ice, saving the long chilly trek. Chris wasn't quite ready for that just yet.

He opened the canvas bag that lay on the ice and took out an ice fishing tent. It was easy for one man to erect, and Chris dragged it over the holes he had drilled and secured the edges with tent stakes driven into the ice. He placed his fishing gear, including a couple of folding stools and the cooler, inside and sat down to prepare his fishing rod. He was enjoying the solitude for now.

The temperature was in the teens when Chris had arrived this morning and wouldn't get much above the twenties during the day. If the wind came up, then the chill factor would be considerably colder: the tent made ice fishing a little more comfortable. The ice fishing huts that were more or less permanent wintertime structures in places like Minnesota didn't work very well in this part of the Rockies; there were storage limitations on the public land surrounding the reservoirs, and wooden huts were expensive to build and maintain. The tents used here were light, inexpensive, and portable and were stored at home in the off season. They could be warmed with small propane heaters.

Chris gazed out of the tent flap toward the vehicle parking area, then turned his attention to baiting the short fishing pole. He lowered the baited hook to the bottom, some thirty feet below, and tied the thin rope attached to the end of the handle of the pole to the leg of his stool—he had lost a pole some years ago when a hard strike from what was likely a large trout had yanked his pole into the water—that wouldn't happen again.

He poured some coffee out of a thermos jug and sipped the hot liquid gratefully as he continued his vigil through the tent flap. Another vehicle had just parked on the lake shore, and a figure exited the truck and disappeared behind its bed. The bearded man reappeared between the trucks, towing a sled similar to Chris's, and began the hike across the ice.

As he towed the sled near the tent, he said, "That you, Chris?"

He was a large man, appearing even larger in his quilted coveralls and sheepskin hat. He was a little winded, his breath visible with each exhalation.

Chris came out to help offload fishing gear, drawing off his glove and offering a hand.

"Mornin', Sam. How was the trip? Snow not too bad up north? Roads were pretty much clear down our way."

Sam Edwards took the offered hand, then towed his sled a little closer to the tent and began piling fishing gear and a cooler on the ice near the tent flap. "We got a light snow last night near Copper Town…none to speak of. Plenty of snowpack on the roads, though. Slow going. Sorry I'm late."

"No matter," Chris replied with a smile. "We've got all day, and the fish are a captive audience." He glanced inside the tent at the fishing pole. "Just got here myself. No bites yet."

Chris went into the tent, followed by Sam. Chris sat down and checked his fishing pole. Sam sat down too and opened his tackle box to prepare his rod. "Thanks for the invite, Chris. I haven't been ice fishing in a while."

"Yeah, the quiet is good for the soul. I guess we're all spoiled, living up here where we do, but even so, the wintertime frozen lakes are special." Chris reached down and jigged his fishing rod a couple of times. "Anyway, you're welcome…been too long since we got out here together."

"I can use a little peace and quiet," said Sam, gazing intently into the hole in the ice into which his fishing line was deployed. "The eight-to-five routine isn't very satisfying these days. Not sure why. Not sleeping very well either."

"Yep," said Chris. "Day-to-day stuff can wear a guy out. Sometimes, it's hard to figure out what's missing."

Sam fiddled with his fishing rod for a moment. He cranked his reel a few turns, then released the bail, permitting the weighted hook to go back to the bottom. He lifted the tip of the rod a few times, jigging the bait, then put the rod back on the ice.

"Thinking about some kind of getaway. Scared. Ashamed. Can't imagine what something like that would do to Mary and the kids… damn!"

Chris reeled in his fishing line, inspected the bare hook. "Must be frustrating. Guess we've all had that feeling that there must be more. Hmm, hard to catch a fish with no bait."

He scooped some bait out of a jar, rolled it into a ball between his palms, and mashed it around the hook. He once again lowered the line into the water.

Sam shifted in his chair and stretched his legs. "Bad news is that some kind of quick fix to feel good can hurt other people…people that don't deserve it."

Chris glanced at Sam briefly, then back at the tip of his fishing rod. "Uh-huh. Lots of temptations out there. Can't forget your promises, though. Part of being a man, I guess. Still, it is hard to know how to deal with routine." Chris coughed out a brief chuckle. "Face it, Sam, being married is hard work, and sometimes, it's a pain in the tail. Maybe there's ways to bring back some fun in your life? Maybe separate the grind from your family?"

Chris's rod tip dipped twice, then plunged into the hole in the ice. He grabbed the pole before it disappeared in the water and jerked the tip upward, setting the hook, then slowly cranked the open-faced reel, initially losing as much as he gained with the light setting on the drag, gradually bringing in the fish. The trout ran with the line a few times, slowly tiring out as Chris steadily retrieved the line. When the fish was near the bottom of the hole, clearly exhausted, Chris pulled off his mitten, put his bare hand into the hole, and flipped the fish up onto the ice.

"Nice cutbow," he said, nodding, grinning widely. "It'll go eighteen, maybe nineteen inches. Rachel will be happy. Loves her pink-meat trout."

He extracted the hook with a pair of needle-nose pliers and tossed the fish outside the tent on the shady side. He kicked some snow over the fish and returned to the tent.

Sam popped the top on a can of Coke, took a sip, and placed the can beside his folding chair. Chris rebaited his hook and sent the hook to the bottom. Sam jigged his rod again.

"Got a problem, Chris. There's a lady. She's an equipment rep who comes by the office every week or two. We've been makin' eyes at each other for a while now. Nothing else…I mean, we haven't sat down to eat yet, but the table's set."

Chris stared at Sam for a long moment, eyebrows raised. "You're not seriously thinking about something like that, are you? You have an awful lot to lose, and one of the most important things is your self-respect."

"Yeah, I know, Chris. I need something to make me feel good, though. I don't have that at home right now, and I don't know why. Don't know if it will ever come back."

Sam took another sip of his Coke, frowning, and wound his reel a couple of turns.

"Damn sure won't come back without some serious effort. You'll want to remember your vows and maybe have a talk with your pastor." Chris gazed into the hole in the ice, then stared at Sam. "You don't want to dishonor yourself, your wife, or the other woman, not to mention maybe forever poisoning the well with your kids. Dammit, Sam, get a grip!"

Sam's face grew long and serious. "You ever been through something like this, Chris?" His voice was rising. "No kids, no dull routine, no temptations? Never been bored and tired out with the same old stuff? Never been pissed at the trap you're in?"

Sam reeled in his line, picked up his tackle box and cooler, shaking his head, and ducked out of the tent flap. He threw his gear in his sled and trudged away toward his truck without looking back. Chris stepped out of the tent and watched his friend walk away. He resisted the effort to call out, to say something to make Sam come back.

*****

Chris walked into the parish office and nodded at the secretary seated at the desk in front of a small stained-glass window.

Caroline was her name, and she smiled with recognition as Chris approached. She was what Chris's mother would have described as pleasantly plump and was possessed of a sweet and kindly nature. She had the perfect personality for a priest's secretary: a mother and a grandmother and an energetic vigor. The local parish had perhaps a thousand members. Father Joe was a small-town parish priest who was able to care for his parishioners with serious attention and still have time for hunting, fishing, and hiking. He was a happy man. He was Chris's priest. He was Chris's partner in outdoor activities. He was also, in a departure from usual Roman Catholic tradition, though perhaps not established doctrine, Chris's friend.

"Hello, sweet Caroline. Can I see Father Joe, or do I need to make an appointment?"

"Well, Chris, he's either working on his homily for Sunday or he's tying flies…hard to tell with him sometimes. I sometimes wonder if he pursues both activities with equal religious fervor," Caroline said with a mischievous smile.

"You want to announce me, or should I just barge in and goof up his authorship or his artistry, as the case may be?"

Caroline smirked. "You know very well that you'd have a hard time messing up either one…go on in."

Chris approached the large heavy door into Father Joe's office. He rapped on the door three times, waited a count of four, then twisted the knob.

Father Joe was a small man, dwarfed by the huge desk that he sat behind. He was peering through professional quality optical loupes at the fly that he was tying. The hook of the fly was held in the jaws of a fly-tying vise which was temporarily clamped to the edge of the desk; bright lights above his head and to his left provided adequate illumination. He calmly raised his head and flipped up the hinged optical device that was strapped around his head. He squinted at Chris, smiled, and shut off both of the lights that were over his project.

"I was about to apply glue and a feather when you hammered on my door," he said with mock outrage. "What's so all fired important that Caroline couldn't ring the phone buzzer?"

They played out a similar scenario whenever Chris came to visit: Chris the intruder, Caroline the inept amanuensis, and Father Joe the victim. All three enjoyed the drama.

"Well, Padre, I came to beg forgiveness for me and for a friend. Your office isn't a confessional, but since I'll be asking about a buddy, I thought that this venue would be more relaxed."

Chris pointed to a chair in front of Father Joe's desk and, when Father Joe nodded, sat down.

"Good time of year to be fly-fishing, you know?" said Father Joe. "The damned tourists are finally back home in Austin or New Orleans or wherever the dickens they come from. The browns are slow to rise this time of year, but there's always a patch of open water somewhere along the river, and without a thousand competitors, fishing is fun again." Father Joe unclamped the vise from the edge of his desk and placed it on the surface to his right. He folded his hands, elbows on the desk. "Anyway, I guess you're not here to talk fishing. What's going on with your pal?"

"He's got some family problems, seven-year itch or midlife jim-jams or something like that. Whatever the cause, I'm afraid that he's going to wind up chasing a skirt. 'Spoze that always makes things worse. I told him so when he brought up the possibility. Just pissed him off. He left in a huff. Not even sure that he'll want to talk to me again anytime soon." Chris looked down, frowned, looked back at Father Joe. "You often caution against being judgmental, but when I heard what Sam was thinking about, I kind of overreacted, I guess. Now I don't know what to say to him, if I even get a chance."

Father Joe leaned back in his chair and folded his left arm across his chest. He put his right elbow on his left hand and held his chin in the web between his right thumb and forefinger. He gazed out the window to his right, organizing his thoughts.

"Your friend is unique, like all of us are, Chris, but the situation that he's found himself in isn't unusual at all. Mix up dull routine, day-to-day stresses, and some temptation, and voila! The recipe for a life-changing mistake is complete." He placed his forearms on his desk and leaned forward, forehead wrinkled, looking straight at Chris. "He needs mental toughness right now and to remember his commitment to his wife, his responsibility to his whole family, and his sense of right and wrong, whether it is faith based or not. Churchgoers have the advantage of a faith that does one of the things that our parents made us do, and that is to behave 'because they said so.' Christians have Abba to turn to for the same advice. Doesn't always work, but that's God's plan. The built-in habit of blind obedience to authority buys time for one's intellectual dissection of what he is doing or thinking about doing."

Father Joe shifted in his chair a little and leaned back, placing his forearms on the arms of his chair.

"Don't be too hard on yourself for annoying your buddy. Sometimes, it takes a whack in the face to get someone's attention. He's hurting, I'm sure, but his hurting is personal, private, sort of selfish until you intruded. You've forced him to realize that his thoughts about reneging on his vows affects lots of other people, not to mention his family. Now he knows that aggravating a friend is in the mix too, and one friend is the least of it." He pointed to a bookshelf stuffed with books, magazines, and folders. "Part of seminary is psychology studies. We need some of that sort of training to permit us to council more effectively, especially because we are celibate. The kind of problem that your friend is having is usually accompanied by depression, and depression has been described by some psychiatrists as the ultimate in self-indulgence. Shaking someone out of that sort of inward turning, that constant self-reference to the exclusion of all else, is a very important part of their counseling and an absolutely imperative part of their recovery. You've started that process for your buddy, and it may not work. Some people don't want to let go of their solipsism."

"Hold on, Padre. That's a little deep for me. What's solipsism?"

"Loosely defined, solipsism is the philosophical position that only the self can be known and, derivatively, that only the self matters." Father Joe pursed his lips and gave a brief shake of his head. "Think self-indulgence on steroids. We all have evidence of it sometimes, but our realization of our place within community in general and within relationships with others specifically usually wins out, eventually. The trick in cases like this one is to stimulate that awareness before bad mistakes are made. Your friend needs a wake-up call." Father Joe leaned forward and stared intently at Chris. "Now, don't put too much of a trip on yourself, Chris. You can try to help, and as a friend, you should do so. But try to remember that efforts like this sometimes fail. Otherwise, nobody would ever get divorced. Appeal to his better nature if you can, but be ready to drop it if it becomes obvious that it's not working."

Chris nodded and looked at the floor briefly, then back at Father Joe as he got up to leave.

"Well, Padre, you gave me what I asked for. Now I have to figure out what to do with it." He smiled and extended his hand. "Thanks," he said, as Father Joe took the offered hand. "Wish me luck or say a prayer, whichever feels right," he said with a wry smile.

Father Joe slapped him on the back as he turned for the door. "I'll do both. Let's go wet a hook sometime, huh?"

Chris nodded and opened the door.

*****

Sam was seated at his desk in a small office near the warehouse. He had been the assistant manager for the building supply company for five years now. He had worked his way up from a lumberyard worker followed by sales agent and had his eye on higher level management, though the advancement was taking longer than he had wished. The business degree that he had earned from the state college might yet pay off.

The first task that he had to tackle after returning from lunch was going through a sheaf of purchase orders, matching them with delivery statements for the month-end inventory and budget meeting the following day. He sighed and found his coffee cup nearly hidden on the cluttered desk. He went to the coffee maker on the cabinet by the window, looking out into the sales area. His secretary's desk was right outside his door where she was seated in her rolling office chair, telephone trapped between cheek and shoulder, writing furiously on a steno pad.

She was probably recording more information that he would need for his report tomorrow. She hung up the phone and finished writing on the pad. Picking up a thick manila envelope from the corner of her desk, she placed the steno pad on top and rose from her chair, turning toward his office door. She knocked, three sharp raps, and waited.

"Come on in, Charlene," said Sam.

She opened the door, leaving it ajar, and walked into Sam's office.

Charlene was almost as tall as Sam and lean as a broom straw. She was ten years Sam's senior and had worked at the building supply company since she had gotten out of high school. She had bright, intense blue eyes and the easy grace of movement that unusually competent people often have.

"Here's the inventory data that you asked for this morning. No surprises. Looks like sales are up from last year, even if it is wintertime. Guess some folks are still building. I can get specifics on whether its inside finishing stuff that's boosting sales if you like?" She moved some papers on Sam's desk aside and put the steno pad in the vacant space. She held up the manila envelope. "This was on my desk when I got back from a smoke break this morning. Forgot about it 'til you got back from lunch. It's got your name on it and a 'personal and confidential' line below." She stared at Sam momentarily as she handed him the envelope and said, "Hope it's something you want to see."

She looked over her glasses at him, gave a curt nod, and turned toward the door.

Sam put down his coffee cup, said "Thanks, Charlene" to the retreating figure, and turned the envelope over in his hands. Closing the door, he returned to his desk and sat down. He pulled a sliding shelf out of his desk front and put the envelope down. Sipping his coffee, he gazed at the envelope with a sense of foreboding.

Taking a letter opener out of his center desk drawer, he slit the flap end of the envelope. The contents were a stack of photographs, maybe ten or fifteen of them. He laid them on the shelf again with trembling hands as he recognized the top photo. It was a faded color picture of Sam and Mary at their high school senior prom. They were smiling, happy, and so very young. Sam stifled a sob as he picked up the photo. Next was a picture of Sam and Mary in a canoe, both in swimsuits. It was taken on one of the river excursions that they had taken with their friends the summer after their college freshman year. He shuffled through the remaining pictures with tears in his eyes. There were shots of their wedding, Mary holding their newborn son, Mary playing dolls with their daughter, Sam and his son wearing baseball uniforms, Sam's son wearing a Boy Scout uniform, and both kids at vacation Bible school. All of the pictures were originals, and there was nothing else in the envelope. Sam knew. There was only one person other than Mary that could have these photos.

Sam dropped the sheaf of photos on top the envelope and sat back in his chair. He gazed at the ceiling through watery eyes and chewed on his lip. He started as his intercom buzzed. Charlene's voice in monotone said, "DeWalt tool rep here to see you."

Sam paused a moment, keeping his back to the window, pressed the intercom transmit button and said, "Send her over to George in Purchasing, Charlene. He can take care of any orders that we might need."

"10-4," said Charlene.

Sam kept his back to the window and leaned back in his chair, fingering his coffee cup, gazing at the framed picture of his wife and children hanging on the wall opposite his desk. He picked up the phone and entered his home number.

*****

May in the Rockies can be warm and dry or snowy and cold. This particular mid-month Saturday was 68 degrees at noon with the remarkably blue, clear mountain skies. The ceremony had been held at Mary's and Sam's church in the center of town. It was an old Baptist church whose membership was large and had more young people and children than any other church in the area. The renewal of vows ceremony was simple and well attended. Sam was surprised at the number of people that joined their celebration and confided to Mary that he didn't know that they had so many friends. Mary had gazed at him in a loving sort of wonder and nodded knowingly. The last few months had been hectic in a good sort of way for them. They had resumed their date nights once or twice a week, something that they did before the kids came along, but which had gradually fallen by the wayside. Family outings including the kids had become near-weekly events too. Sam found that picnics, camping trips, and fishing excursions were pastimes that he had been missing. He stayed busy at work and was involved at home. He was pleasantly tired every night and slept soundly. He was happy.

The reception was being held at the local community center. Mary and Sam arrived after most of the guests were already inside. Sam held the door for Mary and waved at the crowd's applause as they mingled with the guests. He spotted Chris standing near the refreshment table and nodded in his direction. Chris smiled and waved, then crossed the room. He offered his hand.

"Congratulations, Sam. You two look happy."

"Yeah, we are. We've found something that was missing, something important. Something priceless." Sam looked down and shuffled a foot. "Sounds like a chick flick, doesn't it?"

He blushed and chuckled.

Chris pursed his lips. "Well, maybe, but true and certainly worth the effort. Rachel and I are glad for you."

Sam smiled and said, "Appreciate you, Chris, I sure needed your help."

"Right, Sam. Sometimes, a guy just need a nudge."

Chris punched Sam gently on the shoulder and turned toward the door.

Wind, Water, and Mountain

The two lakes were oriented east-west, the smaller west-ernmost lake narrowing at its west end, fed at that point by a large stream that descended between two mountain masses. The saddle between the two mountains was crossed by a highway, a pass to a valley further west. The easternmost lake was five miles long and two miles wide, terminating on its east end in a man-made dam. The two lakes were joined by a narrow waterway. Water egress from the spillways beneath the dam went into culverts under the highway that ran alongside the river.

The prevailing wind around these lakes was north or northwest, but occasional williwaws could blow down the mountains from any direction, unpredictably, through the saddle, and eddy around the surface of the lakes.

The altitude of the lakes was nine thousand feet, so they froze solid in the winter. One- or two-foot-thick ice could easily support the ice fishermen, the snowmobilers, the cross-country skiers, and even full-sized cars and trucks. The lakes were used for boating recreation from ice-off in May until ice-on in November.

The catamaran sailed across the large easternmost lake on a beam reach in a twelve-knot wind, course roughly due east. The lone occupant of the boat had his hands full controlling tiller extension, mainsail, and jib while leaning out over the windward hull, feet tucked under a hiking strap that ran fore and aft on each side of the canvas trampoline that served as a deck. He had the sails trimmed perfectly, and because the breeze was steady today, he could relax a little and enjoy the ride. This boat was designed for a crew of two when it was used for class racing, but Chris was sailing for fun; it was the only sail craft on the lake. Owing to the shallow draft of the boat and to the absence of shoals in the deep water, he had no potential hazards to avoid until he reached the shore.

He kept an eye on the gathering clouds in the mountain pass behind him. Thunderstorms many miles away could generate irregular and gusty wind patterns that would make sailing difficult, and sudden wind shifts and gusts could capsize the boat. Not likely today, though. The wind was steady, and he was headed to the shore where his vehicle and trailer were located.

The boat weighed about 350 pounds, so it was easy to manage on a relatively flat shore area. The mast was twenty-six feet tall and could easily be lowered, stowed, and transported in a cradle on the specially designed trailer.

He beached the boat, the wind driving it twenty feet onto the mixed sandy and rocky shore, as he loosened the sails, spilling air, allowing them to flutter in the breeze. Lowering the sails, he rolled them neatly and carried them over to the trailer which had a long skinny box mounted low and in the center. He flipped up the door on the box and deposited the sails. Returning to the boat, he disconnected the tiller extension and stowed it in the box too.

The mast could be taken down by one person using an ingenious technique by way of a temporarily placed clevis pin in a hinge at the mast base and using the boom as a lever to lower the mast once the stays had been released. Chris removed the pin, tied down the halyards, lowered the spar, and set it on the ground near the trailer. Using a winch mounted on the trailer, he secured the hook at the end of the wire rope to the boat and winched it aboard the trailer. Strapping down the hulls and placing the mast on its cradle, the securing of the sail craft was complete. The whole procedure had taken less than a half hour. He took the cooler off its specially designed rack and fished a soft drink out of the ice.

A fisherman who had been watching the procedure from one of the seats of a fishing boat, which was perched on the trailer hitched to his pickup truck, climbed down and approached.

"Guess you've done that before," he said, smiling broadly.

He was a medium-sized older man wearing bib overalls, brogans, checked wool shirt, and a beat-up bill cap. He had weathered skin and muscular forearms ending in thick callused hands. His eyes were pale blue and perpetually squinting.

"Yep, once or twice," answered Chris. "It's a fairly easy thing to do on this kind of shore here, where I can get my trailer close to the water. Otherwise, takes several guys to pick the boat up and carry it to the trailer. Did you do any good today?" he asked, nodding at the fishing boat.

"Yeah, got my limit." The man shook his head slowly with a mournful smile. "Can't say much for the size of 'em, though."

"Well, they all fry up the same," Chris said with a chuckle. "Least my wife says so. She'll eat all the trout I can bring home"

The man gazed at the sailboat again and said, "You can have what I got today if you want." He looked down and shuffled his feet. "But like I said…ain't much to 'em."

Chris smiled at him. "Thanks, neighbor, but I have a freezer full. Take those guys home to your family."

"It's just me and the grandkids." He looked up and smiled at Chris. "They're good kids…in school today…only reason I got out this morning."

Chris finished strapping down the hulls to the trailer.

"Something about getting out on the water that settles a fella down, doesn't it?"

"Yeah, that's a fact. Even better when I can bring the kids with me. They're old enough now to stay put in the boat…don't worry so much about 'em goin' for an accidental swim."

Chris tied off the mast in its cradle. "Bet the young 'uns love it. Have you got 'em fishing yet?"

"Well, they're only eight and ten, but the boy will reel one in every once in a while. His little sister will hold a pole." He looked down and chuckled, shuffling his foot again. "But her heart ain't in it. Still haven't got her to bait her hook yet. Soon, she'll be wantin' to water ski."

He gazed at his fishing boat, expression turning distant.

"Different kinda boat than the one I was on back in the sixties. Spent a year or so patrolling the Delta. Can't say there was much fun in that." He shook off the thought, turning to Chris again. "Got that little fishin' boat a few years ago, 'bout the time the kids were born. Figured I'd be wantin' to do somethin' with 'em on weekends. Turned out to be a good idea. Wore the motor out once…had it rebuilt. Only good for four or five months or so in the summer, but it's fun for the kids."

"Must be great, watching the little ones grow up. My wife and I haven't been blessed with children yet." Chris shook the hull of the catamaran that was nearest him. It was well secured to the trailer. "Got a bunch of nephews, though, so we get to see a little of it."

The old man kicked at a clump of dirt near his foot, his smile fading. "Well, not everybody is blessed that way, and some that are ain't cut out for it. My daughter just wudn't meant to be a mom, and her old man wudn't any better as a dad." He glanced up at Chris, then toward the mountains, expression thoughtful. "The kids and me do fine, though." He took a deep breath and let out a long sigh. His expression softened. "Sure am glad to have 'em."

Chris looked at his watch and moved toward the old man, offering his hand. "My name is Chris Walker. I'll look forward to seeing you and the youngsters down here sometime."

The old man took the offered hand.

"Jeb Hattfield," he said, with a smile. "I'd like to have those kids watch you drive that funny-looking boat sometime."

Chris laughed heartily, slapped the man gently on the shoulder, and turned toward his truck.

*****

They had decided to go sailing on this Saturday, in spite of perhaps a little more wind than they would usually have liked, but they hadn't been out for a couple of weeks, and the summer boating season would be ending soon. The lake wasn't crowded, so sailing would be safe.

Chris and Rachel, his wife, had been out for about an hour, furiously sailing up and down the lake, squeezing every speck of speed out of the catamaran. The midafternoon sun was dropping, so the temperature was falling a little. The wetsuit tops that each of them wore weren't quite warm enough now. Time to go in. They tacked the boat, putting the tiller over, smoothly moving crab-like, under the boom, to the other side of the trampoline, and sheeting in the mainsail and jib, continuing the close reach toward the shore near the trailer parking area and the loading ramp. The windward hull abruptly rose a little in response to a gust of wind, and Chris eased the mainsheet a few inches, causing the hull to slowly come down, just kissing the water surface. Keeping the boat moving as fast as possible for wind conditions and course of sail required nearly continuous adjustments of rudder position and sail tension and of body position, their weight being ballast, constantly changing parameters of stability. Catamarans were fast, exhilarating, and extraordinarily unforgiving; race courses in even moderate winds were littered with capsized boats. Keeping the boat in "trim" for maximum speed was an art gradually learned and always full of surprises.

Chris ran the boat up on the beach not far from his trailer, easing the sheets, permitting the sails to luff as he and Rachel got off. A little boy and slightly smaller girl were standing nearby watching their every move. The little girl was blond haired and blue eyed. She was dressed for summer in the mountains with shorts and sneakers, a long-sleeved T-shirt and a floppy brimmed hat. Sunscreen glistened on her buttermilk skin, and there was a gob of zinc oxide on her nose. The little boy wore long pants and a T-shirt like his sister's, and his hat and sneakers looked like they were purchased from the same store. Sprigs of unruly red hair jutted out from under his hat. He had a matching zinc oxide–smeared nose.

The little girl walked toward Rachel.

"What kind of boat is that?" she asked, eyes wide. "I never saw nuthin' like that before." She peered at the stern of the boat where Rachel was raising and securing the rudders. "Where's the motor?" She looked up at Rachel, then back at the sailboat, then at Chris. "What'r those cloth things hangin' up there?" She pointed at the sails. "They look like sheets!" she exclaimed in awe.

Rachel laughed softly, smiling down at the little girl. "Aren't you a curious little chatterbox, sweetheart? What's your name?"

Jeb Hattfield walked through the low willows onto the beach and stood by the little girl. "Her name's Emma Lee. That boy over there is her brother Noah…my grandkids." He nodded at Chris, turned back to Rachel. "You must be Chris's wife. I'm Jeb Hattfield."

Rachel walked around the stern of the sailboat and extended her hand.

"I'm Rachel," she said as Jeb took the offered hand. "You've got a sweet little girl here, don't you?" she said as she bent at the waist and offered her hand to Emma Lee.

Emma Lee took a step backward, glanced at Jeb, and seeing the approving nod, approached Rachel and put out her tiny hand. "Pleased to meet you, ma'am," she said with a shy smile. She quickly turned her attention to the boat again. "What's that word?" she asked, pointing to the Hobie logo on the hull.

"That's the name of the company that made the boat." Rachel pointed at the fishing boat nearby, sitting on a trailer in the parking lot just beyond the willows. "Sort of like 'Glasstron' on the side of that fishing boat over there."

Noah joined the three standing by the sailboat.

"It's just a name, Emma Lee…kinda like Chevy or Ford," he said, looking up for approval first at Jeb, then at Rachel.

"Right," said Rachel. She looked at Jeb. "Couple of smart kids here."

"Yep," said Jeb with a flicker of a smile. "Guess they got it from their grandma. She was one smart cookie. College and all…" He looked down, smile fading, then back to his grandson. He scrubbed the little boy's head with his knuckles, gently, smile returning. "They sure didn't get it from my side of the family."

Chris walked around the bow of the boat where he had been loosening halyards and lowering sails. "Hi, Jeb. Good to see you again. These must be the kids you told me about?"

Jeb nodded and repeated the introductions. Both children were eager to take Chris's offered hand.

"Can I climb on your boat?" Emma Lee said, gazing in thrall at the Hobie.

Chris nodded and lifted her onto the trampoline. She crawled over to the mast and stood up, then took a couple of tentative bounces on the trampoline. She smiled broadly, then crawled under the boom to the other side of the boat, coming to her feet again and wandering aft toward the stern, gazing with wonder at the tiller bar connecting the rudders.

"It's a funny-looking boat, and I still can't see the motor."

Rachel walked around the stern of the boat. "This is called a sailboat, and the wind is what makes it go. It doesn't need a motor. Sort of like flying a kite."

"Can I ride on your boat?" asked Emma Lee. "I promise not to fall in the water."

She vowed solemnly. Noah didn't look quite so sure.

"Well, it's getting late, honey, and the wind is blowing kind of hard," Rachel answered with a gentle smile. "Maybe if we get a warm day without too much wind and your grandpa says okay, we can try it." She looked at Jeb, then at Chris. "Think we can make sailors out of these two?"

Chris thought for a moment. "Yep, we could get them on the boat over there." He pointed to the cove near the east end of the lake; it curved around into the north shore near the pier and concrete loading ramp. "Stays pretty calm, and the pier would make it easy to load up the kids." He glanced toward Jeb. "Depends on what Grandpa says, and it depends on the weather."

Jeb helped Emma Lee get down from the boat. "Yeah, I'd like to see the young 'uns give it a shot." He looked at Rachel. "Give us a call when you have time and when the weatherman says the wind won't be blowin' too hard. We'll meet you down here…maybe bring a picnic lunch."

Rachel got her purse out of a waterproof bag tied to the trampoline of the boat and took out a notepad and pen. She wrote her name and phone number down on a sheet of the pad, tore it off, and handed it to Jeb. She took down his phone number, and they said their goodbyes.

*****

The Saturday morning started off overcast and chilly on the lakes, but by nine o'clock, the sky had cleared, the wind was blowing a little under ten miles an hour, and the temperature was seventy-two—perfect sailing weather. Chris had called Jeb and asked if this day was a good time to put the kids on the catamaran. Jeb had enthusiastically assented.

They were gathered at the lakeside by ten o'clock, the children dressed as they had been when last they had visited, except today, each wore a life jacket. They were wide eyed with excitement.

Chris launched the boat and rigged the sails and running gear. Rachel checked the security of the children's life jackets and kept them busy with a brief lesson on what made a sailboat go. They were in awe and mostly uncomprehending, but attentive and fascinated. Emma Lee asked questions nonstop while Noah listened, eyes alert.

Chris finished his preparations and called Rachel and the children to the boat, now fully rigged and tied up to the pier, sails flapping in the breeze.

Chris helped Noah and Emma Lee aboard the catamaran and situated one on each side of the boat. A hiking strap extended the length of the trampoline on each side, and the children were instructed to hold on tight to those straps. He and Rachel untied the boat and pushed the bow away from the pier, letting the breeze fill the jib, blowing the boat downwind. Chris set the rudders and sheeted in the mainsail a little; the little boat gained speed.

Jeb stood on the pier with his hands in his pockets, watching the boat move away. When the children yelled out to him, he waved his right hand, then put it back in his pocket. He turned and walked toward the shore area and sat down in a folding chair by a picnic table that had a cooler and a basket on it.

The catamaran rounded the rocks at the mouth of the cove and pointed closer to the wind, Chris and Rachel adjusting the sails for the new course. The boat picked up speed, and the windward hull rose slightly. The children squealed with delight mixed with anxiety, roller-coaster phenomenon, as they felt the apparent wind on their faces. They were trying to look everywhere at once.

There was a slight hiss as the hulls cut through the water. Emma Lee squealed again as a bit of spray splashed on her cheek and a shoulder.

"It's so quiet!" she exclaimed.

"Yeah," said Rachel. "That's one reason we like it so much. It's fast and exhilarating, but peaceful."

"What's 'exhilarating'?" asked Noah as he tried to look at the direction they were sailing, the sails, Chris controlling the tiller and mainsheet, and at his sister all at once.

"Means 'exciting' or 'thrilling'…kind of like having fun in a hurry." She was watching their course and turned toward Chris. "Fishing boat trolling to port on collision course, maybe one hundred yards. Don't think he sees us and I bet he doesn't see many sailboats out here."

Chris sheeted out the mainsail and let the boat fall off to leeward, bringing it well to the starboard side of the fishing boat.

"Right. Folks that have never been around blowboats before don't know that they have the right of way."

They passed the fishing boat maybe forty or fifty feet away and waved at the startled skipper who had just turned his attention from his trolling lures and noticed them. He waved and flashed a grin as did his two passengers.

"That thing doesn't make much noise, does it? Couldn't hear you coming."

"We're sailing!" bragged Emma Lee as she squirmed about the trampoline.

"Yes, you are," said the fishing-boat skipper. "Looks like you're having a ball."

Chris and Rachel laughed and brought the boat into the wind, slowly coming about and assuming a new course. They sailed up and down the lake for an hour or so, and when the kids started looking bored, they headed back toward the cove.

They eased the catamaran alongside the pier, spilling air from the sails as needed to slow the boat and still maintain steerage. Rachel and the children got onto the pier and headed toward the picnic tables while Chris de-rigged the boat.

By the time that he had the boat loaded on its trailer and parked away from the launching area, Rachel, Jeb, and the children had a picnic lunch spread out on the wooden table near the shore. Noah and Emma Lee were telling Jeb all about their experience when Chris arrived.

"Well, Jeb, I guess the kids like sailing. What do you think?" he asked.

"Reckon so," said Jeb, smearing mayonnaise over slices of bread and dropping bologna and cheese on them.

There were some peanut butter and jelly sandwiches for the children that Jeb had made at home. The children were intently studying the plates holding their lunches and under the watchful eyes of Jeb, resisting the urge to devour their PBJs.

"Hold on, kids, I'm almost done with the grown-ups' food."

Rachel was putting ice in plastic cups and filling them with iced tea. Chris busied himself by passing around forks for the potato salad.

"Looks like we're ready," said Jeb. "Go ahead and give thanks, kids."

Emma Lee and Noah each put their hands together, and together, they softly intoned, "God is great, God is good. Let us thank Him for our food. By His hands, we all are fed. Give us, Lord, our daily bread. Amen."

"Pitch in, kids," said Jeb with a chuckle.

Chris finished chewing a mouthful of sandwich and said, "I think the kids like sailing, but I'm afraid that they got a little bored."

"Maybe," said Rachel, "but wait until they are controlling the boat and the wind picks up. Wind and water have a way of getting your attention." She noticed Jeb's curious expression and said, "I don't see nature as an actively hostile force, but it is indifferent. It can make you humble in a hurry."

"Looked to me like you were controlling the boat real good. Didn't look dangerous at all, least not from my easy chair on the shore," said Jeb with a grin.

"We almost ran over another boat," said Emma Lee, eyes wide.

Jeb looked questioningly at Chris.

"We passed that guy safely. He just wasn't expecting a sailboat," Chris said. "One of the things you learn to like about sailing is that it's so quiet. But you have to keep a sharp lookout for other boats for just that reason."

"Sure looked close to me!" said Emma Lee.

"Don't talk with your mouth full, honey. You'll spatter us with peanut butter and jelly," said Jeb.

Emma Lee giggled and covered her mouth.

"Sailboats have the right of way over power boats, according to standard navigation rules, but smudge pot drivers who never see sailboats and haven't had a safe boating course may not know that." Chris took a sip of tea. "Anyway, the smart sailor will keep a sharp eye out." Chris looked at Emma Lee and Noah. "Remember, kids, always watch where you're going."

Jeb's eyes crinkled as he laughed. "I'd say that's a pretty good idea anytime."

Rachel looked at Chris, smiling. She nodded subtly. "Yeah, sure is."

"Jeb, what do you say about getting the kids some sailing lessons?" said Chris, wiping his mouth. "There's a big reservoir north of here that has a small yacht club. It offers lessons to kids in the summertime. Rachel and I belong to the club, so we could get the lessons without breaking the bank. 'Course there'd be a little driving involved, but Rachel and I drive over there once or twice a week anyway, so it wouldn't be any trouble at all getting the kids there." Chris glanced at the kids, then at Jeb "Anyway, we have 'til next summer to decide…plenty of time to think about it."

"Does lessons mean that we can learn how to sail one of those funny-looking boats all by ourselves?" blurted Emma Lee, eyes huge.

Jeb smiled at the little girl and mussed her hair. "It sure does, honey. We'll take a little while to decide if we have the money to pay for it. It'd be expecting a lot to ask Rachel and Chris to drive you over there. 'Course I could do it on Saturdays, but the rest of the week, I have a job. We'll just have to see." He looked at Chris with raised eyebrows. "Don't know about this, Chris, but we can talk about it some more."

Chris glanced at Rachel who nodded subtly, then back at Jeb. "That's all I can ask."

*****

Rachel, Chris, and Jeb sat on the front row of folding chairs under an awning which protected them from the late summer afternoon sunshine. Bright light glinted off the lake behind them. Along the lakeshore were a dozen or so small sailboats, pulled high up on the sand, their sails flapping gently in the light air. Jeb, Rachel, and Chris, along with other parents and friends, were observing a presentation ceremony. The low dais in front of them had twenty or so folding chairs facing the audience. They were occupied by children of various ages. The commodore of the yacht club stood at a podium beside the children and was speaking into a handheld microphone, announcing the names of the children who had completed the pram sailing lessons. He was preparing to announce the winners of the "fun race" that had been completed just before the presentation ceremony. He called two children, a third place boy and a second place girl, to his podium and gave them medals strung on red, white, and blue ribbons. He motioned them to the side and said, "And the winner of the twelfth annual Children's Pram Race is…" He paused a moment for effect. "Noah Hatfield!"

The audience dutifully applauded as Noah got up from his chair and nervously approached the podium to receive his medal. The presenter placed the ribbon over his head and, taking his shoulders, turned him toward the audience. Noah grinned self-consciously and waved at his grandfather who waved back, as did Rachel and Chris. He returned to his seat, grinning, clutching the medal hanging around his neck.

The commodore addressed the audience again. "We have a new category of accomplishment to present today. As any sailor can tell you, some people who learn how to sail start off slowly, develop expertise gradually, and finally become proficient. Our choice for the first annual Most Improved Sailor goes to Emma Lee Hatfield. Come on up here, Emma Lee."

She squealed, bounded to her feet, and skipped to the podium.

"Wow!" she crowed. "I'm getting a medal!" as she capered before the commodore.

The audience laughed and cheered uproariously. She danced off the dais and ran to the open arms of her grandfather. His eyes glistened as he hugged the little girl.

The commodore laughed into the microphone. "Our presentations are concluded. Let's all go to the clubhouse for lunch!"

The audience stood and greeted the children that dispersed among them.

Jeb hugged Noah as he came near and took a close look at his medal.

"Well, aren't you somethin', Noah?" He hugged Emma Lee in his other arm. "Sure am proud of you two." He glanced at Rachel and Chris, then back at the children. "When I said hello to that guy with that funny-looking boat last year, I never thought it'd come to this."

"I didn't either," said Chris, but sure am glad you did, Jeb. Your kids have been a real pleasure for Rachel and me."

"You're the godparents that they never had," said Jeb. He looked down and shuffled his feet. "Glad you're in their lives."

"Hear, hear!" said Chris. "Let's go eat."

About the Author

Edward "Bud" Melton is a retired professional living in the Colorado Mountains where he engages in the same activities that his primary character, Chris Walker, enjoys in his adventures.

Printed in the USA
CPSIA information can be obtained
at www.ICGtesting.com
CBHW031817221124
17856CB00011B/226

9 798893 092110